Keeping Our Eyes c

..........Are we there yet? ? ?

Lessons from the Exodus

"It was by faith that Moses left the land of Egypt, not fearing the king's anger. He kept right on going because he kept his eyes on the one who is invisible."
Hebrews 11:27

Thank you to my dear friend, and editor, Sondra Spotts. You bring clarity and "editing correctness" to my thoughts. But even more, you remind me and hold me accountable to what God is calling and leading me in while "partnering with Him." Love and appreciate you mucho!!

Thank you to my husband, Bill who encourages and supports while leading us together in sharing the Gospel of Jesus Christ.

Thank you to all my friends who "lent" their stories for this study: Thelma, Candace, Sue-Ellen, Tammy, Kathy, Lori, Bethany, Patty, and Tina.

Unless otherwise indicated, all Scripture quotations are taken from the *Holy Bible*, New Living Translation, copyright ©1996, 2004. Used by permission of Tyndale House Publishers, Inc., Carol Stream, Illinois 60188. All rights reserved.

Scripture quotations marked NIV are taken from the HOLY BIBLE, NEW INTERNATIONAL VERSION,® Copyright© 1973,1978,1984 International Bible Society. Used by permission of Zondervan Publishing House.

For more information please visit: www.kaywray.com

TABLE OF CONTENTS

Chapter One
Plagued Hearts...Jeremiah 17:5-10

Oh Lord, you have examined my heart and know
everything about me.
Psalm 139:1

Aren't we there yet??

Once when we were travelling from Harrisburg, PA, to Chicago, IL, the Chicago airport was not letting any planes land. Instead, they had to circle the airport. We would not have had enough fuel to circle endlessly, so our pilot landed in Indiana to wait for clearance. A couple on the plane were grumbling....to which the pilot replied, " I'd rather be down here wishing I was up there than up there wishing I was down here!"

I have said that phrase many times since in different situations. I think it has great spiritual significance as well. P.S. Everyone made his connections because all the other connections were late as well.

Thelma VE

The account of Pharaoh and the plagues in Exodus has always been fascinating to me. If we look in-depth we will see a direct correlation to our struggles with God and where He "fits" in our lives today.

Pharaoh and the plagues bear evidence that the heart of mankind has not changed since the beginning of time. Solomon wrote in Ecclesiastes "there is nothing new under the sun"...we just tend to rename actions and sins, in order to either justify them or make them seem more appealing.

> "Pharaoh will try to avoid God through procrastination, compromise, and insincere repentance. With each attempt at resisting God, Pharaoh's heart gets harder, until he is unmoved by even the threat of death to his people." [1]

Jeremiah 17:5-10 reveals three things about the human heart:
I. Cursed are those who put their trust in mere humans, who rely on human strength and turn their hearts away from the Lord. They are like stunted shrubs in the desert, with no hope for the future. They will live in the barren wilderness.

The Israelites had been in bondage for over 400 years. Exodus 2:23-25 tells us the Israelites *"groaned under their burden of slavery; cried out for help, and their God heard their groaning. He remembered his covenant promise to Abraham, Isaac, and*

---

[1] The Daily Bible In Chronological Order 365 Daily Readings by F. LaGard Smith, © 1984 by Harvest House Publishers Eugene, Oregon 97402

Jacob; looked down on the people of Israel and knew it was time to act."

Since God spoke the world into existence, surely He could just speak or reach down from heaven and in one felled swoop rescue the Israelites out of bondage and deliver them to the Promised Land!! However, this is not an exercise of creation but rather God using His creation (via Moses and Aaron) to bring about a miraculous story of redemption, deliverance, provision, and promises fulfilled that will affect not only the Israelites but will reach throughout the course of time and impact all of humanity via another Redeemer and Deliverer...Jesus Christ!

Through the struggles of the Israelites in this first deliverance, we will also be able to see in the parallels of our own cry for deliverance. God used a man, Moses, to bring about the Israelites' deliverance. Through the Israelites' journey we will see the temptation and the fallacy of putting our trust in man rather than God.

In Exodus 3 God called Moses to lead His people out of Egypt, and Moses used every excuse he could think of not to be that leader. In all fairness to Moses, stop and think of the daunting task God was giving him! This magnitude of deliverance had never been done before.

Moses is to return to a nation he grew up in as a Hebrew adopted into an Egyptian household, and not just as any Egyptian but in Pharaoh's household of privilege. This wasn't a stranger he was returning to but family that he was supposed to be the voice of reasoning and negotiations. Let's face it, it's easier being a voice to strangers than family! He's returning to a ruler, Pharaoh, who tried to kill him because Moses killed an Egyptian who was beating a fellow Hebrew.

"Who am I to appear before Pharaoh? Who am I to lead the people out of Egypt?" (Exodus 3:11) God quickly set him straight and said "I...not you Moses...I will be with you, I will lead you...I will send you." Right before this God had already identified himself as the GOD of his forefathers, Abraham, Isaac, and Jacob. God is sending him...Period! It will not be in Moses' strength, might, power, or wisdom but in God's. Yes, Moses was the vehicle God would use, but it was always GOD!

Through some pretty impressive miracles the people of Israel were convinced that God had sent Moses and Aaron (Exodus 4:31). However, it wasn't long until the people turned on Moses and Aaron and blamed them for Pharaoh's decision to bring even more hardship on them. The foreman said to Moses, *"May the Lord judge and punish you for making us stink before Pharaoh and his officials. You have put a sword into their hands, and excuse to kill us!"* (Exodus 5:21)

Just as Jeremiah said, **Cursed are those who put their trust in mere humans, who rely on human strength and turn their hearts away from the Lord,** Moses told them God had sent him, but the people were putting their hope and trust in Moses, a mere human being.

I get that! For over 400 years every move they made was orchestrated and dictated to them by a man. Then when Moses performed the first miraculous signs, *"the people were convinced that the Lord has sent Moses and Aaron. When they heard the Lord was concerned about them and had seen their misery, they bowed down and worshiped." (Exodus 4:31)*

But the hope that had risen out of broken and desperate hearts didn't have time to take root until it was tested for both Moses and Aaron and the people.

Moses and Aaron were only to be "the voice" of God to a people who said they wanted change but weren't anticipating to experience the pain of change; to a people who became too discouraged because the promise of deliverance was not seen immediately in this first attempt.

The people refused to listen, and their discouragement and disbelief were contagious, infecting even Moses. Moses lamented to God, "God why have you brought even more trouble to them...thought you said (promised) you were going to deliver, heal, etc.?" (Exodus 5:22, 6:1)

When the Lord told Moses to go back to pharaoh and tell him to let the people go, Moses objected. *"But Lord! My own people won't listen to me anymore. How can I expect Pharoah to listen? I'm such a clumsy speaker!" (Exodus 6:12)*

"I am...I will...I have" (Exodus 6:2-9) God repeats over and over again in this section. Like a gentle but firm reminder to Moses that he cannot and will not be what only God can be to the Israelites.

How many times do we get bent out of shape because we stand on God's Word and promises and God doesn't "deliver the goods" in our timing? We are left feeling foolish and give in to the pressure of "maybe God's promises aren't for today...maybe I didn't really hear God." (Exodus 6:13: "God COMMANDED them to bring the Israelites out.")

We, like the Israelites, will have to stop looking at circumstances, which are very visible, and trust in the "One Who is invisible." (Hebrews 11:27)

Has this ever happened to you...

You may have been praying the same prayer for years hoping, expecting God to move. Silence deafening, eyes growing weary looking for a deliverer. "God, where are You?"

Now, what if the answer comes through a person, through the hands of the person praying for you? You sense something different in your body as soon as they touch you. The next time you need healing, will you seek God or the one who prayed for you?

Several years ago I went with a friend to a famous evangelist's church in another state because she felt if she went there she would be healed. But the healing never came. Did she not hear clearly from God? Did the evangelist not hear or obey? I don't know. I just know I witnessed the pain in her eyes and her body when the healing didn't take place.

What if it's a word of knowledge that no one else would know but God, and that word comes through a person? Would you seek that person the next time you need a specific word?

Or perhaps you have been used by God to reveal an answer to someone. How has that affected you the next time that person comes to you for an answer?

I would think Moses' confidence in what he was going to do was boosted a bit when the elders witnessed the miraculous signs he did before them. "The people of Israel were convinced that the Lord had sent Moses and Aaron." Until Pharaoh was confronted by Moses and he punished the Israelites through heavier demands. (Exodus 5:6-19)

Moses went back to the Lord defeated. "Why have you done this to your people...why did you send me...why have you not rescued your people NOW!"

The point, the hiccup—danger in our faith walk is we all have the tendency to look to a person, the vehicle through which God moved for our answer especially if that person was used to give us an answer before.

Whoever God uses, and it could be you or I, we don't own the path of the miracle. We must always keep our eyes, and likewise point others to the Source, not the vehicle.

II. Blessed are those who trust in the Lord and have made the Lord their hope and confidence. They are like trees planted along a river bank, with roots that reach deep into the water...are not bothered by the heat or long months of drought. Their leaves stay green and they never stop producing fruit.

When Moses protested to God, "Who am I to appear before Pharaoh? Who am I to lead the people of Israel out of Egypt?" God answered, "I will be with you. And this is your sign that I am the one who has sent you: when you have brought the people out of Egypt, you will worship God at this very mountain." (Exodus 3:11-12)

Notice there was no flashing lightning rod or horrendous thunder. No angelic visit. *Just* a burning bush with a voice speaking from the middle of the burning bush that really wasn't burning at all! You know, the "everyday-kind-of-miracle!" The sign that God was going to be with him was going to happen much later...and isn't that the very meaning of trust, of faith, and of hope?

Exodus 7:1-7 is the only place I know of where God told a human being he would make them *seem* like God to another human. This must have had quite an impact on Moses resolve because in verse 6 "Moses and Aaron did just as the Lord commanded them." The more Pharaoh resisted, the stronger their resolve became.

Their "roots of trust" were growing deeper into the river of God! Their hope and confidence was no longer in themselves but branching and attaching deeper into God.

Is this not how Jesus has called us to live today?
"He who dwells in the shelter of the Most High will rest in the shadow of the Almighty. I will say of the Lord, he is my refuge and my fortress, my God, in whom I trust." (Psalms 91:1-2 NIV)
In Hebrew dwells means "to remain, stay". Is this not what Jesus requires of us today? He is the vine, we are the branches, we are to remain in Him. We can not produce fruit on our own. Without remaining, staying attached to Jesus (feeding on His "sap," Word), we too will ask as Moses did, "but how can I...who am I."
When we accept what and where our position should be, then like Moses God will say to us, "Partner with me, I will lead you, I will be with you." (1 Corinthians 1:9) It is only when we *remain attached* to the vine that we can bear fruit; be obedient; remain in His love; be filled with joy in fact, overflow with joy; love each other; and the Father will grant what we ask for using Jesus' name (John 15:1-17).

This world is full of opportunities for us to show the glory of God and like Moses and Aaron, God is asking us, "Will you trust ME? Will you partner with ME? Will you follow ME?"
Trust. A deep meandering of our roots placed in the One, the Only God Who produces hope and confidence.
Trust. A deep meandering of our roots placed in the One, the Only God Who will remain firm in the droughts and storms that come

into our lives threatening to blow us over at our core. But because we are rooted in The One...The Only we can withstand.

Trust. Everlasting spring of living water flowing through us holding us so we can be productive even in the midst of storms.

Through every plague God brought on the Egyptians, God's power, His protection, and His deliverance was beginning to be seen by the Israelites. Especially when the land of Goshen where the Israelites lived went unscathed by the plagues. Can you imagine the fear that gripped their hearts on the night of the first Passover? The heart wrenching cries over the firstborn son of every Egyptian household dying while their firstborn sons were sitting full of life by their sides?

The awesome reality of God! The awesome reality of trust!

III. The human heart is the most deceitful of all things, and desperately wicked. Who really knows how bad it is? But I, the Lord, search all hearts and examine secret motives. I give all people their due rewards, according to what their actions deserve.

That sounds like a pretty bleak state to be in! You might be tempted to throw your hands in the air and say, "what's the point of trying?" And you are correct! In and of ourselves we can make quite a mess of things and get ourselves into a lot of trouble and situations that can bring great heart ache all because of the conditions of our hearts.

Have you ever found yourself saying something then questioning, "where in the world did that come from? Why did I even say that? What is in my heart that would make me respond or react that way? That's not me or perhaps the 'me' I think I am"!

The plagues were a direct result of the condition of Pharaoh's hardened heart in response to Moses' request to let the Israelites "make a three day journey into the wilderness to offer sacrifices to God." (Exodus 5:1-3).

God used the plagues to cement His power and His protection in the minds of a people that would definitely need to trust this God when they left Egypt.

Time after time we read in Exodus 7:14-10:27, "Pharaoh's heart is stubborn...Pharaoh's heart remains hard...He refused to listen." His own magicians exclaimed, "This is the finger of God!" Yet his heart remained hard and stubborn.

Then we read in Exodus 9:12, "But the Lord hardened Pharaoh's heart." Wait a minute. Why did God harden Pharaoh's heart? That doesn't sound fair!

Let's analyze the scripture with scripture. What do we know about God's character? Psalms 103:7, "He revealed his character to Moses." What did God reveal about His character? Listed below are some but not an exhaustive list of God's character from Psalm 103:

- Forgives my sin

- Heals my diseases
- Redeems me from death
- Crowns me with love and tender mercies
- Fills my life with good things
- Compassionate and merciful
- Slow to get angry
- Filled with unfailing love
- Will not constantly accuse us, nor remain angry forever
- Does not punish us for our sins; nor deal harshly with us as we deserve
- His unfailing love has no limits and remains forever
- Tender and compassionate to those who fear him
- He has removed our sins as far as the east is from the west

He remembers our sins no more (Isaiah 43:25)

He takes no pleasure in the death of the wicked (Ezekiel 18:23; 33:11)

Does not want anyone to be destroyed but everyone to repent (2 Peter 3:9)

His patience gives people time to be saved (2 Peter 3:15)

His justice is pure and true (Psalm 103:6; Isaiah 11:1-5)

He will never go back on his Word (Isaiah 45:23)

The Bible reveals His character: just, loving, truthful, holy, shows compassion, mercy, grace, judges sin yet offers forgiveness to name a few. He is revealed as "the Supreme Being; the Creator and Ruler of all that is;

the Self-existent One perfect in power, goodness and wisdom. God is One, but exists as three Persons--Father, Son and Holy Spirit--and each has specific roles yet are united. God is Spirit, infinite, unchanging, exists everywhere...at the same time, has ALL power and authority which is recognized as such by others whether in "heaven, earth or beneath the earth." We cannot understand God apart from His works, because what God does flows from who He is. God became incarnate, the Son of God became the Son of Man restoring relationship of mankind to God. It is only through the Son that we can have forgiveness of sins, reconciliation with God, and eternal salvation.

Correct thinking about God prevents false idolatrous ideas of who He is. Psalm 50:21 "When you did these things and I kept silent, you thought I was exactly like you. But I now arraign you and set my accusations before you."[2]

Character is defined as "a distinctive mark, trait or quality, status, position." God's self proclamation of His character, "I AM

[2] Got Questions.org "Who is God?"

and there IS no other god; there is none like me!" in Isaiah 46:9, defines "a distinctive mark, trait or quality, status, position."

God's response to Job and his accusatory friends in Job chapters 38-41 clearly defines God's "distinctive mark, trait or quality, status, position."

We can not categorize God in order to make Him fit into our human concept of fairness or justice. Nor can we judge God's actions based on human expectations.

God chooses people according to his purposes; he calls people, but not according to their good or bad works....Are we saying, then, that God was unfair? Of course not! For God said to Moses, "I will show mercy to anyone I choose, and I will show compassion to anyone I choose." So it is God who decides to show mercy. We can neither choose it nor work for it. For the Scriptures say that God told Pharaoh, "I have appointed you for the very purpose of displaying my power in you and to spread my fame throughout the earth." So you see, God chooses to show mercy to some, and he chooses to harden the hearts of others so they refuse to listen. Well then, you might say, "Why does God blame people for not responding? Haven't they simply done what he makes them do?" No, don't say that. Who are you, a mere human being, to argue with God? Should the thing that was created say to the one who created it, "Why have you made me like this?" When a potter makes jars out of clay, doesn't he have a right to use the same lump of clay to make one jar for decoration and another to throw garbage into? In the same way, even though God has the right to show his anger and his power, he is very patient with those on whom his anger falls, who are destined for destruction." (Romans 9:16-22) "As surely as I live, declares the sovereign Lord, I take no pleasure in the death of the wicked, but rather that they turn from their evil ways and live." (Ezekiel 33:11)

In the Garden of Eden, Genesis chapters 1-3 prior to the invasion of sin, it was God who set the boundaries and consequences for Adam and Eve. They were the ones who chose to disobey and sin. God, like any good parent, simply implemented the consequences of their disobedience, which by the way, they were warned of in advance. Through their actions and choices, Adam and Eve, not God, severed the relationship with God. However, it was God Who provided the Avenue by which that relationship would be restored. God's heart was and is always bent to restoration with His children, His creation. But He will not forsake, will not compromise Who He is for restoration to be fulfilled in your heart or mine.

"Concerning the Gentiles, God says in the prophecy of Hosea (2:23) 'Those who were not my people, I will call my people. And I will love those whom I did not love before'." (Romans 9:25)

We may question God's fairness, but had it not been for His justice and mercy toward us that bore out as judgment on the body of His Son Jesus Christ at his crucifixion, we would not have the undeserved privilege of being called His child! Of being given the free gift of salvation, restoration, hope, and life!

We deserved the penalty for our sins...He took our place!

We deserved death...He gave us His life!

> *"He never sinned, nor ever deceived anyone. He did not retaliate when he was insulted, nor threaten revenge when he suffered. He left his case in the hands of God, who always judges fairly. He personally carried our sins in his body on the cross so that we can be dead to sin and live for what is right. By his wounds you are healed."* (1 Peter 2:22-24)

Was this fair for Jesus Christ? Absolutely not!

Fairness was not the motive or the end result...the love of God was!

What about our hearts today?

> *"These people say they are mine. They honor me with their lips, but their hearts are far from me. And their worship of me is nothing but man-made rules learned by rote." (Isaiah 29:13)*

I pray this may not be said of you and me!

> *"And I will give you a new heart, and I will put a new spirit in you. I will take out your stony, stubborn heart and give you a tender, responsive heart. And I will put my spirit in you so that you will follow my decrees and be careful to obey my regulations."* (Ezekiel 36:26-27)

How's your heart? Do you want a tender responsive heart? Moses warned the Israelites before they went into the Promised Land:

"This command I am giving you today, and it is not too difficult for you to understand and it is not beyond your reach. No, the message is very close at hand; it is on your lips and in your heart so that you can obey it. Today I have given you the choice between life and death, between blessings and curses. Oh, that you would choose life, so that you and your descendants might live! You can make this choice by loving the Lord your God, obeying him, and committing yourself firmly to him. This is the key to your life." (Deuteronomy 30:11,14, 19-20)

The message of the cross, of salvation, has never been too difficult to understand or beyond anyone's reach.

"If you confess with your mouth that Jesus is Lord and believe in your heart that God raised him from the dead, you will be saved. For it is by believing in your heart that you are made right with God, and it is by confessing with your mouth that you were saved....Jew and Gentile are the same in this respect . They have the same Lord who gives generously to all who call on him. For everyone who calls on the name of the Lord will be saved." (Romans 10:9-13)

I pray you have responded to this message of salvation...to life.

HOMEWORK = link between what we have <u>learned</u> and what we <u>think</u> about, which results in what we put into <u>practice</u>

What progression do these verses show in keeping our hearts pure and focused on God?

Psalm 90:14,17

Psalm 91:1-4

Psalm 101:2-3

Chapter Two
Call to Worship-Dressed for Worship...Exodus 34:14

*Praise the Lord! Let all that I am praise the Lord. I will praise the
Lord as long as I live. I will sing praises to my God with my dying
breath.*
Psalm 146:1-2

*Come, let us bow down and worship, let us kneel before the Lord
our maker;*
*for he is our God. We are the people of his pasture, the flock
under his care.*
Psalm 95:6-7

Aren't we there yet??

Curt and I planned to visit my aging grandparents in
Oklahoma, so we climbed in my parents van along with my 12
year old sister in California to drive the 25 hours to Enid,
Oklahoma. We had a wonderful visit with family and left a few
days later because we were desperate to be back in our
church for Easter services. Somewhere around Albuquerque,
New Mexico, we had engine trouble that delayed us for a long
day. After driving all night we got off the highway for
breakfast and drove to the top of the hill just as the sun
popped up and the song, "I'll rise again" played!! We felt the
Holy Spirit and genuine joy from our Lord and Savior!   Best
Easter ever!!

Candace H

Worship.

Webster defines worship as "Intense love or admiration of any kind. Something worshipped."

The worshipper will always take on the character of that which he worships.

Think about it. People have imitated and dressed like Madonna, Michael Jackson, Elvis Presley, The Beatles. There is a whole culture of men who have assumed the physical identity of Elvis!

Worship is a word that is thrown around in both the secular and religious arenas. Throughout history kings and rulers have set themselves up as objects of worship. The rich and famous, political figures (and at times all too willingly), have become objects of our worship. Religious figures and styles have been the focus of worship. Music has been the focus of worship. Churches have been the focus of worship.

The Israelites were only days out of Egypt when they transferred worship of God to worship of a golden calf. Did you ever wonder why a calf? Calf worship was a part of religious worship of almost all the ancient people of their time. Bulls were worshiped in Egypt. The Israelites witnessed and were inundated with this worship for over 400 years.

Although they just came out of slavery in Egypt, they are still living a part of their slavery to the past. The slavery they would now have to be set free from was not a physical state imposed upon them but would entail a deliverance their minds and spirits had yet to experience.

Pagan cultures in the Old Testament used sexually induced atmospheres as a form of worship to their fertility gods. Many shrines and temples had temple prostitutes available for their worshippers. Drug-induced trances were used to contact their gods.

The Israelites took on the character of the gods they worshipped, which led them to do despicable things to themselves and one another. They performed sexual obscenities in worship of the fertility gods; their children were sacrificed to appease the gods even though God forbade such demonic practices.

> *"Do not permit any of your children to be offered as a sacrifice to Molech, for you must not bring shame on the name of your God. I am the Lord." (Leviticus 18:21)*

In fact, it was in this type of atmosphere where Jesus took His disciples to ask them, "Who do you say that I am?" in Matthew 16:13-20, Mark 8:27-38, and Luke 9:18-36.

Caesarea Philippi for centuries was a center of worship of the heathen god Pan.
According to Wikipedia:

> In ancient Greek religion and mythology, Pan (/pæn/;[1] Ancient Greek: Πάν, Pan) is the god of the wild, shepherds and flocks, nature of

mountain wilds, rustic music and impromptus, and companion of the nymphs.[2] He has the hindquarters, legs, and horns of a goat, in the same manner as a faun or satyr. With his homeland in rustic Arcadia, he is also recognized as the god of fields, groves, wooded glens and often affiliated with sex; because of this, Pan is connected to fertility and the season of spring. The ancient Greeks also considered Pan to be the god of theatrical criticism.[3] The word panic ultimately derives from the god's name.[3]

One of the cities of the Decapolis is said to have been the sight of the Transfiguration. It is in this sight that Jesus prepared His men for His upcoming suffering, death, and the re-adjustments they would be called upon to make as His followers after He was gone. This is where they would learn to cement "Who" He was compared to the gods that were worshipped in their culture.

We must know the "Who" we worship before we can "dress" for the worship.

Worship is a believer's response to God's revelation of himself. It is expressing wonder, awe, and gratitude for the worthiness, the greatness, and the goodness of our Lord. It is the appropriate response to God's person, his

---

[3] https://en.m.wikipedia.org/wiki/Pan_(god)

provision, his power, his promises, and his plan.[4]

It was out of the amazing wonder and awe of being in the very presence of Jehovah that made the Samaritan woman leave her empty jug at the well and return to the village that rejected her to tell them about the Messiah she had just encountered (John 4).

God calls us...wants us...longs for us to worship Him. So much so that He is concerned even about the smallest minute details of our heart's worship.

The details in the blueprints of the Tabernacle, priesthood, and the clothing worn by the priests suggests that no detail of man's worship of God is too minute for God's concern. They speak of the closeness and intimacy of God to His people yet show the great divide between humanity and the deity of God. They speak of the expectations of God and His precise obedience to whatever He commands. They speak of mercy yet judgment. They speak of inclusion of _His_ people and yet exclusion of _His_ people when sin is worshipped.

The Old Testament priests were the only ones ordained and allowed to wear the priestly garments and enter His presence. Today, as New Covenant priests, we too are to dress in worship of God. And just like the High Priest of old, we too are invited to come into the Holy of Holies...in fact we have the

---

[4] A Place of Quiet Rest by Nancy Leigh DeMoss © 2000, pg 211

awesome privilege of "housing" the God of the Holy of Holies right in our hearts today!!

So what are our garments as we live our daily-24 hour-worship today? How do you and I begin our day, our 24 hours?

Jesus our great Teacher, Example setter, opens the door to welcome us into what His days looked like.

> In the morning he taught in the synagogue and delivered a man from an evil spirit; then went to Peter's house where he healed his mother-in-law of a high fever; had lunch (scripture doesn't say but I would imagine Jesus took advantage of the intimate time with Peter's family and James and John to do some one-on-one discipleship); in the evening *"MANY sick and demon possessed people were brought to Jesus. The whole town gathered at the door to watch. So Jesus healed many people who were sick with various diseases, and he cast out many demons." (Mark 1:21-34 capitalization added)*

Phew! I don't know about you, but that's exhausting just reading His action, emotionally filled day!

This is just a glimpse into one day. And remember, their mode of transportation was walking...Jesus couldn't just hop in a car to save time from point A to point B.

His days were filled with physical, spiritual, and mental exhaustion. Anyone who has been part of any ministry will at some point experience some form of exhaustion. There is an exhilaration and heightened sense of awareness of God's Holy Spirit preparing and moving in and through you during ministry. But when you are finished, there comes a letdown, a draining from this heightened sense.

> "Because God's children are human beings – made of flesh and blood – the Son also became flesh and blood. For only as a human being could he die, and only by dying could he break the power of the devil, who had the power of death. Only in this way could he set free all who have lived their lives as slaves to the fear of dying. Therefore, it was necessary for him to be made in every respect like us, his brothers and sisters, so that he could be our merciful and faithful high priest before God. Then he could offer a sacrifice that would take away the sins of the people. Since he himself has gone through suffering and testing, he is able to help us when we are tested. This high priest of ours understands our weaknesses for he faced all the same testings we do, yet he did not sin." (Hebrews 2:14,17; 4:15)

Jesus experienced exhaustion! Think about it. He had just three years to mentor, to live out before his followers the life he was calling them to live before others. These were the public years, yet I would think the other thirty years were filled with preparations for these three years...they weren't years of rest and relaxation.

> "While Jesus was here on earth, he offered prayers and pleadings, with a loud cry and tears, to the one who could rescue him from death. And God heard his prayers

because of his deep reverence for God. Even though Jesus was God's Son, he learned obedience from the things he suffered." (Hebrews 5:7-8)

He had three years to live out faith and trust in God in the midst of persecution, ridicule, misunderstanding and even death. His followers, then and now, would be called to live this same faith and trust.

"If the world hates you, remember that it hated me first. The world would love you as one of its own if you belonged to it, but you are no longer part of the world. I chose you to come out of the world, so it hates you. Do you remember what I told you? 'A slave is not greater than the master.' Since they persecuted me, naturally they will persecute you. And if they listen to me, they would listen to you. They will do all this to you because of me, for they have rejected the One who sent me." (John 15:18-21)

How did He do all He was supposed to accomplish without losing His mind? How did He get "dressed...prepare" for his day?

Jesus knew the key to heeding the call to worship and dressing for worship begins with the preparation and anticipation of worship. David said, *"**Early in the morning** I lay my requests before you and wait expectantly." (Psalm 5:3 bold type added) "Satisfy us **in the morning**, that we may sing for joy and be glad all our days." (Psalm 90:14 bold type added)*

When we enter into worship we must come anticipating the touch of The Master, the voice of The Master and the realization, thanksgiving, and surrender to The Master of our redemption!

*"**Before daybreak** next morning, Jesus **got up** and went out to an **isolated place** to pray." (Mark 1:35 and bold type added)*

I am not the best sleeper, and it never fails if I have to set my alarm, that would be the time I am sound asleep! Our bodies need sleep to rejuvenate and to function. We must also be aware of and listen to our bodies', especially in times of illness and recuperation. When Jesus took on the form of man He was made in every way like us. I can only imagine there were mornings, just like we have, when His body resisted His Spirits need to awaken. And He, like we must, made the choice to start His day preferring His spirits needs over His physical needs.

Jesus taught His disciples in John chapter 15 in order to have the power and ability to live...to produce fruit...to hear and follow in obedience, their quiet times were not an option but the very breath of their souls.

To stay connected to the Source, His Father, He had to initiate that connection when and where no one could interfere with the connection. This was where He would find, not just joy (John 15:11) but overflowing joy; where he would find peace even in the midst of desertion (John 16:31-33); where he would function in love (John 15:9) even in the face of persecution and ridicule.

If we want to know the will of the Father for us, there is no shortcut. We must spend time talking with and listening to the Father.

I am convinced the body of Christ, especially in Western culture, is not unified today because we have become too entangled with the worries of this life, this world, rather than surrendered to the Source of this life. When we do not make it a priority to spend time alone with the Father, we will only be able to offer the world stagnant rather than living water through our silence to the hurting and lost around us. We are to be the light and salt to our culture. The church is not to be a mirror of our culture; rather our culture should be a mirror of the church.

> *"I am praying not only for these disciples but also **for all who will ever believe in me** through their message. I pray that they will all be one, just as you and I are one – as you are in me, Father, and I am in you. And may they be in us so that the world will believe you sent me. I have given them the glory you gave me, so they may be one as we are one. I am in them and you are in me. May they experience such perfect unity that the world will know that you sent to me and that you love them as much as you love me." (John 17:20-23 bold type added)*

Jesus prayed for you and me!

Jesus' purpose for being on this earth was to do the will of the Father. There was no other priority or calling higher than that. Our purpose for being on this earth is to do the will of the Father. There is no other priority or higher calling than that. Everything we do encompasses that very mission. Time alone with God gives us the strength, power, and wisdom as we navigate school, work, relationships, marriage, parenting, and ministry opportunities.

Alone with the Father in the wilderness is where Jesus gained the strength and courage to resist the taunts of Satan's temptations.

In the midst of exhaustion and facing horrendous physical abuse and thoughts of His death on the cross, Jesus gained His strength from time spent with the Father moments before His arrest. This is where he received grace to do the unimaginable and power to do the impossible for you and for me.

Too many times I believe the lie that I can do all things according to "my strength." But in my strength is where I become frazzled, impatient, angry, and annoyed with others interruptions of "my time...my space...my energy."

I realize there will be readers of this book in all seasons of life. Some are just launching into careers after college, some are newlyweds, new parents going on two hours of sleep, growing families with never ending activities, adult children caring for aged parents, grandparents, retirees, unexpected divorce or death of a spouse, etc. Each season of life has time challenges that don't need to sidetrack us from spending time in worship and communication with God.

Your quiet times may be in the middle of the night while feeding an infant or when they nap during the day; perhaps it's moving your lunch break to your car; perhaps it's on your commute to and from work in your car. It's not about the schematics of the "isolated place" for worship but about answering the call to worship no matter where you and I are living...right now.

Whatever stage of life you are in, please take to heart I am not trying to "add" more to your plate. Nor is my purpose in writing this to add guilt. This isn't about a checklist or an obligatory duty. It's not about a specific time allotment because this will also change according to our season of life. It's about worshipping even when we may not "feel" like it!

- It's about God calling us, pursuing us, longing for us because He is our lover, always thinking about us, desiring our company before "our doing."
- It's about our response not out of obligation but out of a heart of gratitude, out of a heart of thanksgiving, out of a heart overflowing with indescribable love and affection for the One who paid it all...forgave it all...accepts us right where we are.
- It's about a heart surrendering even when we don't have the answers or love in doubt.
- It's about a heart desperate for His touch that can restore sanity in the midst of chaos.

- It's about a heart bursting forth in joyful response to the invitation to, "Oh, come let us adore him...Christ the Lord!" Even when we don't feel like it.

HOW DO WE COME DRESSED FOR WORSHIP?

The intense ache in our hearts can only be filled and fully satisfied by the Creator of our heart. We don't come dressed in perfection. The Creator of our hearts lives within us...He knows our hearts are "heavy ladened." When we come dressed in honesty with hurts, exhaustion, pain, dissatisfaction, rejection, sickness, fear, unbelief, and honestly lay them before the Lover of our souls, surrendering to Him, He will then clothe us in His power. He will be our rock, our safety, our protection, and our strength.

We come with hearts dressed in reverence, awe, and respect for Who He is.

"Those who live in the shelter of the Most High will find rest in the shadow of the Almighty. He alone is my refuge, my place of safety; he is my God, and I trust him. He will cover you with his feathers. He will shelter you with his wings. His faithful promises are your armor and protection." (Psalms 91:1-4)

He calls...we answer...He delivers. "Oh come let us adore Him, Christ the Lord" is not just a carol sung at Christmas but the cry of an exposed heart dressed for worship.

HOMEWORK = link between what we have <u>learned</u> and what we <u>think</u> about, which results in what we put into <u>practice</u>

According to John 4:23, what kind of worshipper does the Father seek?

What does "worship in Spirit and in truth" mean to you?

Read Psalm 100. How are we to worship Him?

Notice there is no stipulation of only when we feel like it or when everything is going our way.

Chapter Three
Equipped for Battle-Not Ready...Exodus 13:17-22

"Because he loves me," says the Lord, "I will rescue him; I will
protect him for he acknowledges my name. He will call upon me,
and I will answer him; I will be with him in trouble, I will deliver him
and honor him. With long life I will satisfy him and show him my
salvation."
Psalm 91:14-16 (NIV)

Aren't we there yet??

We were in northern Moldova on a ministry trip. Our
transportation back to Chisinau was a bus from Kiev, Russia.
Finding seats in the rear of the bus we observed that the only
language we had in common with the other passengers was
that of smiles and nods. As night settled we were transfixed
by the darkness: no lights on the road nor in the distance. At
some point the bus came to a grinding halt. Having no idea
what was transpiring, we watched all but three people leave
and simply disappear in the dark of night. We had our
Romanian cell phone, but no number for the Pastor awaiting us
in Chisinau. Never before had we felt this kind of
helplessness. Grabbing hands we prayed. Looking up we saw a
young man approaching. Having no language in common, the
inexplicable happened. He communicated to us the process of
phone code, international code and country code. We began

with a call to Hungary, leading to a call to Romania, resulting in a call to Moldova. The truth of His Word, "You will never be alone for I am always with you," became another living testimony in our lives.

Sue-Ellen E

"When Pharaoh let the people go, God did not lead them on the road through the Philistine country, though that was shorter. For God said, 'if they face war, they might change their minds and return to Egypt' ....the Israelites went up out of Egypt armed for battle." (Exodus 13:17-22 NIV)

Prior to the Israelites leaving Egypt, they had never been faced with fighting as soldiers. They were slaves taking commands, building bricks, and doing menial slave work. In their hearts they may have wanted to kill their Egyptian captors; however, they had neither the skill nor the equipment to be an army.

When they left Egypt they left with a multitude of items to be used in the construction of and worship in the tabernacle. The generation (20 years and older) that left Egypt would eventually die in the wilderness. The next generation that was born and raised in the wilderness would become the soldiers Joshua would lead in the conquest of the promised land.

We live in a world where we don't have the luxury of not being in some form of conflict or battle. Unless we surrender to the enemy we will always live in a state of equipping for battle, being in battle, or in the outcome of the battle.

We must always keep in the forefront of our thoughts that we, just as these Israelites, are aliens living in a world not our home. We are passing through and will be prey for the inhabitants of this world (worldview). Let's not get so comfortable that when faced with adversity we, like the Israelites, "go back to Egypt...surrender to" the world in order to avoid the battle.

What are our marching orders and mission in our sphere of influence today (neighborhood, work, recreational arenas, etc)? There comes a time when we need to "stop crying out to the Lord and move on" as we will see God told Moses!

We can be equipped yet not ready for battle.

The Israelites left Egypt with carts, baskets, anything that could carry the plunder the Egyptians willingly gave them as they began the great exodus. Think about it. Days earlier they were slaves dreaming of freedom. They didn't escape or sneak away under cover. They left in full sight with the blessings from the same people that loathed them. They didn't ransack their homes and steal away with their plunder. All the years of living in loathsome conditions while their taskmasters lived in luxury. Justice for their years of slavery was about to be witnessed and all they had to do was put their hands out to receive it!
Exodus 12:35-36 tells us:

"And the people of Israel did as Moses had instructed; they asked the Egyptians for clothing and articles of silver and gold. The Lord caused the Egyptians to look favorably on the Israelites, and they gave the Israelites whatever they asked for. So they stripped the Egyptians of their wealth!

Exodus 13:18b, *"...the Israelites left Egypt like an army ready for battle."* There is a big difference between wearing a soldiers uniform carrying a gun and actually being a soldier in the midst of a battle.

The Israelites were about to witness God's ability to go before them in battle, a lesson they would desperately need to understand if they were to *get to* the Promised Land and *conquer* the Promised Land. We too will need to learn this lesson as we navigate through this world to get to our Promised Land.

In Exodus 14:2, God directed Moses to turn the Israelites back and camp between Migdol and the sea. One final time God would harden Pharaoh's heart and in regret he would chase after the Israelites to bring them back to captivity and slavery. God's purpose in doing this was, *"I have planned this in order to display my glory through Pharaoh and his whole army. After this the Egyptians will know that I am the Lord! So the Israelites camped there as they were told." (Exodus 14:4)*

In defiance and rage Pharaoh took 600 of the "best of his best" chariots and commanders in pursuit of the Israelites.

Pharaoh caught up with the Israelites and they saw the powerful force of the Egyptian army approaching with no escape route available for them!

Wow! Talk about being between a rock and a hard place!!

The Israelites remembered how the Lord miraculously displayed His power through the plagues in Egypt; how He orchestrated their exodus from Egypt and with ignited faith they cry out, "Do it again Lord...display your power and glory before us!"... NOT!! They panicked and blamed Moses for bringing them out of Egypt (totally forgot they willingly walked out of Egypt....no "pushing" from Moses!); wanted nothing to do with Moses; and proclaimed slavery in Egypt was better than any difficulties in their road to freedom.

In their hearts and minds they had already surrendered to the enemy before the battle began.

- This battle they were about to encounter was more than escaping from the treacherous enslavement of a formidable foe.
- This battle would lay a groundwork for future battles and future conquests.
- This battle would determine the direction of not only their feet's path but their heart and faith path. This battle would be their boot camp...their preparation.

God would first need to equip them for spiritual battle before they could be victorious in physical battle. Again, today we are not so different from the Israelites in their faith journey.

What was Moses' response to the approaching Egyptian army?

...Don't be afraid

...Stand still

...Watch the Lord rescue you (refocus your attention)

...The enemy you see today, you will never see again

...The Lord Himself will fight for you, just stay calm (Exodus 14:13-14)

Fear can paralyze us. I love God's "practical" counsel: "Why are you crying to me?...get moving!" Now in fairness to the Israelites, they didn't <u>see</u> an escape route. The Egyptians were closing in on one side, and the Red Sea was on the other. However, they had just witnessed His miraculous deliverance from Egypt that should have been fresh in their memory banks and burned hope within their hearts. Should have, right?!

Can you remember a time when it seemed you were trapped, hedged in on all sides with no "reasonable" escape (answers)? How did you react?

"*Then the angel of the Lord, who had been leading the people of Israel, moved to the rear of the camp. The pillar of cloud also moved from the front and stood behind them. The cloud settled between the Egyptian and Israelite camps. As darkness fell, the cloud turned to fire, lighting up the night. But the Egyptians and Israelites did not approach each other all night."* (Exodus 14:19-20)

Lessons we can learn:
- God receives the glory THROUGH our enemies 14:18
  Psalms 20:7-8 "Some nations boast of their chariots and horses, but we boast in the name of the Lord our God. Those nations will fall down and collapse, but we will rise up and stand firm."

  Numbers 22, Deuteronomy 23:3-6 the story of Balaam and Balak:

  Balak, the Moabite King, had seen everything the Israelites did to the Amorites and he and his people were terrified at the vastness of the Israelites. The King said, *"This mob will devour everything in sight, like an ox devours grass in the field."*

  So the king hired a diviner named Balaam to curse the Israelites. At Balak's first request Balaam inquired of God and God told him not to go with Balak or to curse the Israelites because they were blessed. Balak doesn't take no for an answer and sends some of his higher ranking officials and better monetary enticement. This time, God permits Balaam to go but cautions him to only speak what he is told. Balak takes Balaam to three different places expecting each time Balaam to curse Israel and all three times Balaam blesses Israel.

- God repositioned himself from front (leading) to back (protecting)
  (Exodus 14:19-20)
  There will be times when God is clearly leading us. Other times He will be protecting us and encouraging us on. Even when we don't "see" Him.

- Our way of escape may not always look the safest
  (Exodus 14:21-25)
  "Trust in the Lord with all your heart; do not depend on your own understanding. Seek his will in all you do, and he will show you which path to take." (Proverbs 3:5-6)

- The enemy knows the Lord is fighting for us.
  (Exodus 14:25; 2 Kings 6:14-23)

- Our fear and trust is redirected to God as a result of our deliverance
  (Exodus 14:30-31)

- Don't forget to praise the Lord "in front of, through, and after" the battle
  (Exodus 15:1-18; 2 Chronicles 20:21-24)

In Judges 2:1-5 we read the Israelites never fully occupied the Promised Land with the freedom the Lord promised because of their unfaithfulness to Him. His promise was that He would go before them...He would be the Victor in their battles. Their part was complete surrender, reliance, obedience, and worship of Him and Him alone-no other gods.

I wonder how many victories we have forfeited today because we want the victory our way. Because we get ahead of God then ask Him to come along as assurance victory will come. Or because we start, walk, and end our day in our power and not His.

Ephesians 6:10-18 tells us how we are to dress for battle everyday. Paul begins this exhortation with, *"Be strong in the Lord and in His mighty power."*

We don't fight a physical foe but a spiritual foe; therefore our strength must come from a spiritual source. *"Therefore, put on the full armor of God, so that when the day of evil comes, you will be able to stand your ground, and after you have done everything, to stand." (NIV)*

> *"For though we live in the world, we do not wage war as the world does. **The weapons we fight with** are not the weapons of the world. On the contrary, they **have divine power to demolish strongholds**. We demolish arguments and every pretension that sets itself up against the knowledge of God, and we take captive every thought to make it obedient to Christ." (2 Corinthians 10:3-5 NIV bold type added)*

44

Like any good soldier we don't wait for the battle to begin getting ready for it. We prepare in advance making sure our "equipment " is ready:

- Belt of Truth (John 17:17-20; John 14:6; John 8:31-32)
- Breastplate of righteousness (Philippians 3:9)
- Shoes of peace (1 Peter 3:11,15-16)
- Shield of faith (Hebrews 11:1,6)
- Helmet of salvation (Romans 12:2; 10:9-13)
- Sword of the Spirit (Hebrews 4:12)
- Prayer (Philippians 4:6; Luke 18:1-8)

Every piece of this armor is based upon and held together by Truth. If we don't know the Truth:

- about Christ's righteousness, not ours;
- about true peace that will carry us even in the midst of conflict;
- about faith even when we can't see;
- about the Word of God as our standard of Truth
- about having a sound mind, not fear, in our salvation; and praying without ceasing...never giving up...our armor, our preparations for battle will fall short in the midst of the battle.

"Standing firm...standing our ground" means we walk in obedience, surrender, and trust in the only One whose power and authority is above those with whom we will be in battle. All other gods, powers, principalities, rulers must surrender to the Lord (Colossians 2:10,14-15,20; Philippians 2:9-11; 1 Peter 3:22).

Let us not be like the seven sons of Sceva in Acts chapter 19 when they tried in their own power and strength to invoke the name of Jesus, Whom they did not know or serve, to attack and fight a spiritual foe. Even spiritual foes know a phony when they see one! The evil spirits replied to these men, "*I know Jesus, and I know Paul, but who are you? Then the man with the evil spirit leaped on them, overpowered them and attacked them with such violence they fled the house naked and battered.*"

We dress to do battle for others

We are not an army of one! As in a physical army we encourage, support, protect those that are in this battle with us, and deliver those under the clutches of demonic forces. Jesus came to seek and to save (Luke 19:10) those who are lost, and that should be our battle cry too.

Isaiah reminds me I not only dress to do battle for myself but "to intervene to help the oppressed."

"Yes, truth is gone, and anyone who renounces evil is attacked. The Lord looked and was displeased to find there was no justice. He was amazed to see that no one intervened to help the oppressed. So he himself stepped in to save them with his strong arm, and his justice sustained him. He put on righteousness as his body armor and placed the helmet of salvation on his head. He clothed himself with a robe of vengeance and wrapped himself in a cloak of divine passion. He will repay his enemies for their evil deeds. His fury will fall on his foes. He will pay them back even to the ends of the earth." (Isaiah 59:15-18)

We take our cue, our orders from the One who has worn the armor, who IS the armor, and found it to be impenetrable. Our armor is secured and held in place by the belt of Truth because the One who has given us this armor, the One who will fight the battles through this Armor IS Truth. He has promised us, *"you will know the truth and the truth will set you free." (John 8:32)*

Our part: submit, believe, trust, remain faithful, and be ready.
> *"Stay alert! Watch out for your great enemy, the devil. He prowls around like a roaring lion, looking for someone to devour. Stand firm against him, and be strong in your faith." (1 Peter 5:8-9)*

HOMEWORK = link between what we have <u>learned</u> and what we <u>think</u> about, which results in what we put into <u>practice</u>

How did Nehemiah build the wall? Nehemiah 4:15-18
We will not always have the opportunity to be in a prayer closet praying without ceasing. There will be times when we are both working and doing battle.

What does God promise us as we go through the battle(s)? Isaiah 43:1-3,13;
Jeremiah 17:5,7-8

Chapter Four
Dangers of Emotional Commitment...Exodus 32-33

Delight yourself in the Lord, and He will give you the desires and petitions of your heart. Commit your way to the Lord; trust in Him also and He will do it.

Psalm 37:4-5 (AMP)

Aren't we there yet??

We recently flew to Roatan, Honduras to visit my grandma. I had been there before but did not have an address saved. It's a small island and I guess addresses aren't necessary. Anyway, the customs official asked for the address where we would be staying and my response was "grandma's house." He kinda chuckled and knew I was serious but didn't really know what to do or say. After a couple of minutes describing how to get to grandma's house, he let us go. There really is no address!

Tammy C

When our commitment to God is more a matter of emotion or a feeling rather than sincere dedication, our obedience and commitment will always be short-lived.

Throughout the book of Psalms David expressed a variety of emotions from anxiety, fear, anger, and depression to unspeakable joy and indescribable love. No matter the circumstances around the writing of each Psalm, David would return to commitment and trust in his God based on truth and not emotion. The truth David relied upon was that God was his defender, protector, up lifter of his soul, provider of all his needs, healer, and restorer, no matter what the circumstances were dictating.

When we allow emotions and feelings to lead us rather than relying on the truth, they can blind us from the reality of what is really going on or from difficult decisions that need to be made in the midst of the circumstance.

We find ourselves in a balancing act with truth and emotions because without emotions we would live as robots. Exodus chapter 32 opens with this foreboding account:

> *When the people saw how long it was taking Moses to come back down the mountain, they gathered around Aaron. "Come on," they said, "make us some gods who can lead us. We don't know what happened to this fellow Moses, who brought us here from the land of Egypt."*

Let's take a quick tour of how quickly the Israelites' memories escaped them:

- Exodus 24:3: Moses went down to the people and repeated all the instructions and regulations the Lord had given him. All the people answered with one voice, "we will do everything the Lord has commanded."

- Exodus 24:7: Then he took the Book of the Covenant and read it aloud to the people. Again they all responded, "we will do everything the Lord has commanded. We will obey."
- Exodus 24:9-14 Then Moses, Aaron, Nadab, Abihu, and the 70 elders of Israel climb up the mountain. God called Moses alone to come up to him. Moses instructed the others to stay behind. Specifically tells them, "if anyone has a dispute, Aaron and Hur are here. They can consult with them."
- And the rest, as they say, "is history."

EMOTIONAL COMMITMENT VERSUS DEDICATION AND OBEDIENCE

In the people's eyes Moses took too long (Moses was only gone for about a month), and their emotional commitment to God is transferred to a golden calf idol that Aaron says "just appeared when the gold jewelry was thrown into the fire!" Wow! Talk about shirking responsibility and accountability!!

A leader can be swayed from making good sound choices when emotional commitment trumps dedication and obedience. Even a religious leader, like Aaron, could be swayed when emotional commitment trumped dedication and obedience.

Aaron led through emotion. It seems he did not want to take a stand and encourage the people to wait for Moses...to wait for what God would reveal to them through Moses.

Moses led through dedication and obedience.

Exodus chapter 32 tells us God responded in anger to His wayward children, and Moses once again had to intercede on their behalf, although Moses also was angry with the people. Moses reminds God of His promise by His oath to Abraham, Isaac, and Jacob when God wants to destroy Israel and make Moses into a great nation. Moses' action on behalf of the people clearly showed his commitment based on truth and not emotion.

I'm sure there were days he thought, "if these stubborn people weren't around it would be so much easier to lead!" We too, in leading those around us to a deeper relationship with God, can say with Moses, "if these people weren't around, ministry would be so much easier!"

I can't help but think through each of these reprimands Moses had to choose between pleasing God...following God...being obedient to God rather than seeking the favor of man or taking the easy way out. And isn't that part of the rub in an emotional commitment? We can get so wrapped up in the moment, in the event, or in the energy of others around us. If we aren't careful, if we lose our footing in truth, we too begin to choose man's opinions over God's. We too choose emotion over truth.

Acts 13 gives the account of a Jewish sorcerer, a false prophet named Bar-Jesus who had "attached himself" (NLT version) to a governor in Cyprus. The governor had invited Paul and Barnabas to visit him because he wanted to hear the Word of God. This sorcerer interfered and tried to keep the governor from believing. Paul, filled with the Holy Spirit, confronted the sorcerer and revealed to him he would become blind, and he did. The governor became a believer as he watched all this transpire.

Interesting phrase, "attached to," because it has everything to do with our commitment to God or someone/thing else. So the question begs, "To whom are you attached/committed?"

To answer this we are going to take a journey into the amazing land of "Word study," which happens to be one of my favorite journeys!

We are going to explore what happens when we attach ourselves to a belief or unbelief, to an emotion/feeling rather than the truth and the toll it will take on our lives physically, emotionally, and spiritually.

WORD STUDY ISAIAH 30:12-18

*"Because you have rejected this message (<u>the message of the Holy One of Israel</u>), **relied** on **oppression** and depended on deceit, this sin will become for you like a high wall, cracked and bulging, that collapses suddenly, in an instant (<u>like a water balloon overfilled</u>). It will break in pieces like pottery, shattered so*

mercilessly that among its pieces not a fragment will be found for
taking coals from a hearth or scooping water out of a cistern."
Isaiah 30:12-14 (NIV bold type and underline added):

1. ADDRESSING THE PROBLEM

RELIED: *Hebrew is 'sha-an' (Shaw-an')*

In the Hebrew this word actually means "to trust in, support, lean, attach." Think of a tomato stock that must be tethered to, attached to, a support so it doesn't fall over.

OPPRESSION: *Hebrew is 'osheq' (o'-shek)*

Means oppression, gained by <u>extortion</u>.

Webster defines extortion: the <u>exaction</u> of too high a price.

(exaction = exacting: "the act of making severe demands of someone; tyrannical; not easily satisfied")

Isaiah is declaring that Judah is attaching itself to oppression and lies rather than relying on God. Isaiah 30:12 could be rephrased as:

<u>"You have 'attached' yourself (sold yourself) to a 'tyrant' that will make severe demands upon you that are not easily satisfied. You have relied on their 'illusions, lies, and deceit' as a way of life. The cost you will pay for this sin will be paid at too high a price. You won't be able to satisfy it."</u>

So what have we attached ourselves to today? Can you name some attitudes or beliefs?

[Example: Pride, Self-pity, anger, tolerance, ignorance, running after philosophies of this culture, addictions, gossip, current 'religious' fads/cults…the word "ifs"; living in the past; or "someday"…living in the future.]

EFFECTS OF UNHEALTHY ATTACHMENTS

- 75 million people (1 in every 3 adults 20+) suffer from high blood pressure (2016 CDC)[5]. 2011 puts total costs in US at $46 billion for health care services, medicines, and work loss costs.
- Worldwide 7 million people die of heart disease and it is the leading cause of death for both men and women[6]
- Millions of people are afflicted with ulcers and stomach problems.[7]
- Panic/anxiety disorder and depression affects 40 million adults in the United States age 18 and older, or 18.1% of the population every year.[8]
- About 70 million people have a sleep disorder.[9]

Everywhere we look today we see signs of overload, stress, and burn-out, in the workplace, at home, and in relationships.

---

[5]https://www.cdc.gov/dhdsp/data_statistics/fact_sheets/fs_bloodpressure.htm

[6] https://www.cdc.gov/heartdisease/facts.htm

[7] https://health.usnews.com/health-conditions/digestive-disorders/peptic-ulcer/overview

[8] https://adaa.org/about-adaa/press-room/facts-statistics

[9] https://my.clevelandclinic.org/health/articles/11429-common-sleep-disorders

According to Mr. Neil Neimark in "The Body Soul Connection"[10]:

"When we experience excessive stress— whether from internal worry or external circumstance—a bodily reaction is triggered, called the 'fight or flight' response. This inborn response prepares the body to 'fight' or 'flee' from perceived attack, harm, or threat to our survival. It was designed to protect us from the proverbial saber tooth tigers that once lurked in the woods and fields around us, threatening our physical survival. Today's saber tooth tigers consist of rush hour traffic, missing a deadline, bouncing a check, or having an argument with our boss or spouse. Nonetheless, these modern day, saber tooth tigers trigger the activation of our fight or flight system as if our physical survival was threatened. On a daily basis, toxic stress hormones flow into our bodies for events that pose no real threat to our *physical* survival.

It is almost impossible to cultivate positive attitudes and beliefs when we are stuck in survival mode. Our heart is not open. Our rational mind is

10 http://www.thebodysoulconnection.com/

disengaged. When we are overwhelmed with excessive stress, our life becomes a series of short-term emergencies. We lose the ability to relax and enjoy the moment. We live from crisis to crisis, with no relief in sight. Burnout is inevitable. This burnout is what usually provides the motivation to change our lives for the better. We are propelled to step back and look at the big picture of our lives—forcing us to examine our beliefs, our values, and our goals."

Moses dealt with burnout. Even Jesus needed to get away...needed to be renewed and refreshed. Many times Jesus left the crowd to go off by himself and be **renewed** by communion with the Father.

Dr. Archibald Hart has said, "Stress management is a spiritual discipline. God expects us to manage our lives responsibly. (I Thessalonians 4:4) We are designed for camel travel—but we continue to behave like supersonic jets."[11]

We have long paid too high a price to these tyrants, and they will never be satisfied. They have had a direct impact upon how or even if we seek God; and because of relying on "their deceit" (what the world tells us if we just live this way...or accept

[11] The Soul Care Bible © 2001 by American Association of Christian Counselors, pg 1568

this attitude) rather than truth, we WILL become rebellious children to God.

Romans 12:2 Don't copy the behavior and customs of this world, but let God transform you into a new person by changing the way you think. Then you will learn to know God's will for you, which is good and pleasing and perfect."

The tyrants we attach ourselves to have a direct impact on our families and their families. The price Christ paid to the "tyrant of sin" so we could rely/attach ourselves to Him was HORRENDOUS! It cost him his life but the "tyrant of sin" was TOTALLY SATISFIED! We don't have to keep paying the tyrant!

If you and I want to hear from God today, then we must "rely...attach" ourselves to Him today and every day.

Isaiah 30:13 "This sin will become for you like a high wall, cracked and bulging, that collapses suddenly, in an instant."

Our tyrants will become for us like a bulging wall. We don't know when...don't know how...don't know what will be the final straw, but IT WILL come crashing down around us and leave us useless. Because our foundation will be based on one untruth upon another, our foundation will not be firm enough to withstand the winds of adversity.

The Word of God is the Truth we are to "attach" ourselves to DAILY.

Deuteronomy 30:11,19-20 (NIV): "Now what I am commanding you today is not too difficult for you or beyond your reach. This day I call heaven and earth as witnesses against you that I have set before you life and death, blessings and curses. Now choose life, so that you and your children may live and that you may love the LORD your God, listen to his voice, and hold (ATTACH) fast to him." (Word in Parentheses added)

2. FINDING THE SOLUTION

This is what the Sovereign LORD, the Holy One of Israel, says:

*"In **repentance** and **rest** is your **salvation**,*

*in **quietness** and **trust** is your **strength**,*

Isaiah 30:15 (NIV bold type added):

REPENTANCE: Hebrew *'shubawh'* (*shoevah*) means "returning"

REST: Hebrew *'abah'* (*ahvah*) means to be willing, to consent, yield to, accept ,to desire

SALVATION: Hebrew *'yasha' (yawshak)* means to be liberated, be saved, be delivered

The beginning of this verse could be rephrased as:

> "In returning from crisis and stress, from relying on lies and deceit... return BACK to relying on God (yielding to and desiring Him), and you will be liberated...delivered from these tyrants of oppression."

QUIETNESS: Hebrew *'nachath'* means "quiet attitude, rest of death =undisturbed calm

> Is there too much "noise" in our lives to hear God speak?
>
> Are we "comfortable" with quiet?

The "rest of death" is a strange concept. There is no activity in death, no listening, speaking...calm...nothing! Undisturbed...PERIOD!

> *"Be STILL and know that I am God." Psalms 46:10...*Let go of anything that is holding me back!

The reality is we find time for that which is a priority to us. We find time to get our hair done, to have our nails done, to shop, to go to the gym, etc. Schedule this "time...rest of death" if you must!

TRUST: Hebrew 'bitchah (beethah)' means trust, confidence "nothing more YOU can do". It speaks of surrender. I need to trust in Someone Who can do in my life what I can't do in and of myself.

STRENGTH: Hebrew 'gebuwrah' means strength, might, power

Using these definitions, the end of this verse could be rephrased as:

> When I become quiet, when I make time, when I surrender all of me, then I come to a place, a person of might of power and of victory in my life who is not tyrannical in exacting a cost that will bring death to me. God came to give life…and life abundantly!

When we give up control and instead trust, take God at His Word (remember trust means "nothing more *I* can do"), then my strength is not dependant on me or my "emotion of the moment" but on God. He will prove his Word in our lives. He can be trusted!

3. SOURCE OF OUR STRENGTH

Paul gives a beautiful picture of what happens when we remember God is the source of our lives:

"But we have this treasure in jars of clay to show that this all-surpassing power is from God and not from us. We are hard pressed on every side, but <u>not crushed</u>; perplexed, but not in despair; persecuted, but not abandoned; struck down, but <u>not destroyed</u>."
(2 Corinthians 4:7-9 NIV underline added)

There is a connection between Isaiah's description of what filled their lives and what Paul says should fill our lives. John 14 describes the Holy Spirit as the Spirit of TRUTH.

John 14:16 (NIV) "And I will ask the Father, and he will give you another counselor to be with you forever—the Spirit of Truth. The world cannot accept him, because it neither sees him nor knows him. But you know him, for he lives WITH you and will be IN YOU."
(Capitalization added)

The difference between Isaiah's description of what was in Israel's "container" (lies, deceit and oppression—those things the "world/Satan" fills us with when we follow him) and Paul's description of what should be in our "containers" is the Spirit of Truth.

ISAIAH (Israel)	PAUL
Relies (attached/filled) on oppression and deceit	Power of God: rely (attach/fill) power of God= liberty and truth
Cracked and bulging	Hard pressed on every SIDE
Collapses suddenly	BUT NOT CRUSHED firm
Completely ABANDONED	foundation Isaiah 7:9
Broken, COMPLETELY DESTROYED	Perplexed, not despair
	Persecuted, not abandoned
	Struck down, NOT DESTROYED

Greater is He that is *WITHIN* us than he that is in the world! Our strength is not dependant on outside forces, on what we attach/rely on. Clay jars are *not* a symbol of strength on the outside. We find the strength is dependent on what it is *in* the jar.

CHARACTERISTICS OF A JAR OF CLAY

CLAY JARS ARE FRAGILE

Busyness is not a substitute for godliness..for the intimate times God longs to have with us. God knows we are fragile. We all:

- Have limits and stress points, and your limits may be different from mine and vice versa
- Need to learn to say "no" at times and not feel guilty for it. It is easier to say "no" to a root canal than something that we enjoy doing. However, if we do not learn to say "no," overload and stress will eventually catch up to us and we will return to being emotionally driven.
- Need to rest and sleep and not feel like we are being lazy for it. Learn what your boundaries are and then stick to

them. Remember Jesus did not heal 24 hours a day. He _made_ time to be with His Father. We were never designed to be the EverReady bunny.

THE POTTER DETERMINES WHAT THE JAR WILL BE USED FOR

- We can "overload" ourselves to the point we will no longer be effective for the purpose for which God created us.
- We don't have to do everything, just the purpose for which God has called us. People wanted Jesus to "perform" miracles. People wanted Jesus to "assume" the role of a king on this earth. But these were not His purpose...not what God had determined why He was born.
- We need also to know that our purpose may have different facets as we go through our lives.
- Consider doing less. Focus on doing what God has called you to do.
- Let the Holy Spirit be the force behind the labor, not guilt, whether your own or someone else trying to impose their guilt on you. The Holy Spirit will accomplish what God had intended, and then He will receive the glory, not us.
- Daily life happens; the unexpected happens. Are you storing up "spiritual food" during times of plenty to be used during times of drought?
- It is God who wants to determine our day, not us, so He can fulfill the purpose He determines for us. But you and I must be ready...we are "in training" to fulfill the purpose He has determined for us. Do I ever miss the mark, miss

the opportunities that He sets before me during the day? Yes and so do you. Repent and move on!

- We need to learn to give our day over to Him at the beginning of the day. God already knows what our day holds for us. We serve Him better when we don't drag our feet and stubbornly stick to our agenda for the day. Ask for discernment to discern divine interruptions and trying-to-get-you-off track interruptions.

"In his heart a man plans his course, but the Lord determines his steps." (Proverbs 16:9 NIV)

"Many are the plans in a man's heart, but it is the Lord's purpose that prevails." (Proverbs 19:21 NIV)

AS THE POTTER SHAPES THE JAR, ONLY THE POTTER CAN SEE WHAT IS INSIDE

God sees inside your heart and mine. We might be able to hide from one another, but we can't hide our hearts from the Potter.

- He made you, you…and He made me, me. Celebrate your uniqueness!
- He sees the heartache and hurts, the secrets we don't think anyone else knows about.
- He hears the "why's," "this just isn't fair" of our lives.
- He sees the potential only God knows we have within us.
- He sees the talents and giftings that He has placed within us.
- He sees the failures, the victories, and the "so-so" times in our lives.

- He sees the journeys of life we have all been through up to today, and He even knows the end of each of our journeys.

And amazingly enough He _still_ has chosen to put His Treasure, His Holy Spirit within this frail and fragile jar of clay! WHY? Because we are to live out our relationship with God in our world so those around us can see "the all surpassing power" to live in our world is not from us but from God living in and through us.

4. LIVING THE PROMISE

Blessed are all who **wait** for him! (Isaiah 30:18 NIV bold type added)

WAIT: Hebrew "chakah" means to tarry, to long for
- How long am I willing to wait, to surrender to the promise rather than the tyranny of the "now?" Forsaking the instant...the quick fix" for the blessing of my promise?
- Do I long for God or do I fill my life; do I over-schedule my life with 'things' rather than wait for the promise of rest? Rest is part of the journey.
- Do I long for God as I long for food when hungry, water when thirsty, and companionship when lonely?
- Am I willing to dig my heels in with God's presence and His timing for direction in my life?
- Am I willing to pledge with Moses:
  > _"...let me know your ways so I may understand you more fully and continue to enjoy your favor...If your_

presence does not go with me (us), do not send me (us) up from here." (Exodus 33:13-16)

- Do I inspire others to wait...to remain in God's presence...in devotion to God rather than "follow me?"

    "Inside the Tent of Meeting, the Lord would speak to Moses face to face, as one speaks to a friend. Afterword Moses would return to the camp, but the young man who assisted him, Joshua son of Nun, would remain behind in the Tent of Meeting." (Exodus 33:11)

"O Lord, be gracious to us; we long for you. Be our strength every morning our salvation in time of distress. He will be the sure foundation for your times, a rich store of salvation and wisdom and knowledge; the fear of the Lord is the key to this treasure." (Isaiah 33:2,6 NIV)

The definition of sin means "to miss the mark" as in an archer missing the red bullseye in the target with his arrow. When we rely on our emotions rather than commitment based on truth and fact, we will always miss the mark in our relationship with God.

The end result of our longing and obedience become God's not ours because it will be based on the truth of His Word. We don't have to make sure everything works out because *"we know that in all things God works for the good of those who love him, who have been called according to His purpose." (Romans 8:28 NIV underline added)*

God is still the same God Who gave the promise to Israel to "remember" He gives to us today. He is the same God Who wants to provide for us today. When we wait on His provisions, His timing, His plan for our life (Jeremiah 29:11), we will not become the "crumbling walls" about which Isaiah warned.

When we wait on Him, it will not be at the cost of our health, our families, and our churches. Deceit and selfishness will not be the foundation that will crumble, because our foundation will be firmly dependent upon His rest, salvation, and strength.

HOMEWORK = link between what we have <u>learned</u> and what we <u>think</u> about, which results in what we put into <u>practice</u>

STANDING STONES

Read Psalm 119:11,33-40. What do these verses say to you about the role God's Word plays in your life?

Throughout the Old Testament the Israelites used "witness stones" of their covenant with God or of something significant that happened in their lives. What reminds you of your covenant with God...your commitment to follow Jesus Christ?

Chapter Five
Fulfillment of the Call...Exodus 17 and 18

A single day in your courts is better than a thousand anywhere else!
I would rather be a gatekeeper in the house of my God than live the good life in the homes of the wicked.
Psalm 84:10

Aren't we there yet??

When my father-in-law passed and we were flying home to Harrisburg, PA, for the funeral, the airline was having some issues, so we were diverted to another city in Oklahoma. We managed to get a flight into Baltimore where we would rent a car, so we thought we were all set. We boarded the plane and noticed our luggage sitting beside the plane all by itself. When we told the flight attendant, she said not to worry, they would get it. About a minute later, we boarded the flight without our luggage. All our dress clothes for the funeral were sitting there and we went on without it! When we got to Baltimore, we came off the plane to see a friend standing there putting her son on that same plane. She offered to give us a ride to Harrisburg, PA, but we declined because we needed a car for the week. When we got to the car rental, we were told they had no cars left because so many people had been diverted to different airports. This was all before everyone had cell phones so we were beside ourselves. The "God Moment" in this is that we were able to get back to our friend at the gate, and we hitched a ride with her. Our luggage arrived sometime after 11pm that night with minimal damage so we did not have to go shopping, and we got to spend time with one of our dear friends on the ride.

Kathy G

Some commentaries say it took 635 years from the time God promised Abraham he would make him into a great nation to the exodus of the Israelites (Abraham's descendants) from Egypt.

It struck me that the anticipation of the promise can be very different from the actual fulfillment of the promise. We can be very enthusiastic and excited about something God has called us to do - excited, energetic, and ready to dive in with the anticipation of the enabling and gifting that we can sense God instilling within us for that promise. However, when the time comes for us to actually *move* in the fulfillment of the promise the full impact can be less than anticipated.

Have you ever felt that way? You get a sense God is stirring within you to do something for Him. You wait and you pray and wait some more and pray some more. Finally you begin to see nuggets of a plan that God is developing, not giving you all the details yet enough for you to realize God is leading you in a certain way, a certain path. And then the time comes and you start walking in what you believe is "the" calling and... IT'S NOT HOW YOU THOUGHT IT WOULD BE!

To be a leader, one must be a servant. Jesus made that very clear when He said that he came not to be served but to serve.

> *Whoever wants to be a leader among you must be your servant, and whoever wants to be first among you must become your slave. For even the Son of Man came not to be served but to serve others and to give his life as a ransom for many. (Matthew 20:26-28)*

We see throughout the Old Testament any leader who was successful, and I mean successful as far as accomplishing great feats for God, had to serve. Serving was his first calling.

- Jacob...served Laban 14 years for his wives
- Joseph...served in Potiphar's house, the prison warden, and Pharaoh.
- David...served King Saul
- Ruth...served Naomi
- Samuel...served Eli
- Moses...served Jethro
- Joshua...served Moses

When I think of Jacob, Joseph, and Moses, ordinary men with flaws whom God called to do great accomplishments for Him, I can't help but think of servitude.

It seems serving is the very road God used to whittle away pride, deceit, and arrogance so they would come full circle in surrender to God and serve with hearts of gratitude rather than selfishness. Serving requires humility. Serving requires obedience even when we don't understand or feel like it.

We come face to face within our own hearts of any entitlement, pride, or arrogance through serving others. God has a funny way of revealing to our hearts what we find irritating in others via the road of service!

Moses was raised in the best and with the best growing up in Pharaoh's home. He was used to being served, having the best of anything he wanted.

When Moses fled into the desert he also ran away from his station and position in life. God was now telling him to go back to face his family, colleagues, friends...his servants as now a servant of God. When God first called him, Moses gave every excuse he could think of to get out of serving God. Moses finally surrendered and returned to Egypt, and God used him in mighty ways to deliver His people from Pharaoh and Egypt.

Entitlement and the call of God should always be viewed in our lives like the mixture of oil and water...that just doesn't happen.

Lessons we can learn:
1. **God knows our abilities and gives accordingly to what we will need**. Hebrews 13:21; 2 Corinthians 3:5,12; 1 Corinthians 2:4; 1 Corinthians 12:4-5, 11, 18

It has been said abilities are natural inbuilt qualities while a skill is learned. Knowledge and ability creates a skill. God gave us those inbuilt abilities when he "knit us together in our mother's womb; He made all our delicate, inner parts; made us wonderfully complex; every day of our lives were recorded in His book; every moment laid out before a single day had passed" as Psalms 139 declares. Simply amazing!!

Knowing this, I can confidently rest in the assurance that whatever calling God is placing on my life, He has already instilled the abilities I will need, and He will give me the skills (gifts) needed to fulfill that calling. All to bring glory and honor to His Name...not mine!

Discovering our abilities usually is a result of trial and error. Trial and error requires a heart of humility and a willingness to make a mistake and learn from it...no matter the negative responses that could come from others.

If you are unsure of what abilities you have:
- Ask the Lord to reveal these to you.
- Seek out a friend who will be honest and encouraging in what they see.
- What do you enjoy doing?
- Resist the urge to depend on your own strength even though it might come "naturally" to you.

In Matthew 25:14-30 is a beautiful illustration of how God gives His gifts "in proportion to their abilities." God also expects responsible return of His invested gifts in us. *"To those who use well what they are given, even more will be given, and they will have an abundance. But from those who do nothing, even what little they have will be taken away."*

Always remember our gifts are not ours to hoard, hide, or boast about but are on loan. God will give us what we *need* to fulfill His calling. Use them wisely so God will receive *all* the honor and glory. Remember, He will not share His glory with anyone.

Each time Moses' abilities and skills were put to a test via the Israelites, his first response was to cry out to the Lord. Likewise, that should be our starting point.

2. **Not everyone is going to welcome our help, gift, or message (sometimes we won't!).** People will complain we aren't doing it right.

   Moses protested his calling to God multiple times, and God assured his calling multiple times in Exodus chapter 3. Moses was told to call the elders together, *"tell them... the God of Abraham, Isaac, and Jacob appeared to me. He told me, I have been watching closely, and I see how the Egyptians are treating you. I have promised to rescue you from your oppression in Egypt. I will lead you to a land flowing with milk and honey..."* (Exodus 3:16-17) even assuring Moses the elders would accept his message

(3:18). God kept it real though and tempered the encouragement with the reality Pharaoh would resist, all for the purpose of God cementing His power and glory in the minds and hearts of the Egyptians and the Israelites.

As we read through the story of the plagues, the exodus from Egypt, and eventual entry into the Promised Land, I have a suspicion Moses' fulfillment of his calling was not what he anticipated. The Israelites went from excitement to fear to anger to complaining and back around again Moses was always at the receiving end. Not only was his leadership questioned, his siblings even mumbled against his wife!

The people grumbled that he wasn't "doing it right" and wanted to return to their slavery, as if that was better!!

Moses' constant reliance on God was going to be the avenue by which he would fulfill his calling even when the voices of those around him would seem louder than God's.

As with Moses, God's calling on our lives will not win a popularity contest from those around us. And with Paul, our approval must not be based on what others think.

> "For we speak as messengers approved by God to be entrusted with the Good News. Our purpose is to please God, not people. He alone examines the motives of our hearts." (1 Thessalonians 2:4)

"Obviously, I'm not trying to win the approval of people, but of God. If pleasing people were my goal, I would not be Christ's servant." (Galatians 1:10)

3. **We cannot "be all things" to everyone** (Exodus 18:13-23). Moses had previously sent Zipporah, his wife, and their two sons back to his father-in-law, Jethro, at some point during Moses and Aaron confronting Pharaoh to let the Israelites leave Egypt. In chapter 18 we read that Jethro brought Zipporah and their children back to Moses. He had heard everything God had done for Moses and how he brought them out of Egypt. When Jethro and Moses meet, it is very clear that Jethro is overwhelmed with praise to God because of what He had done.
The account tells us that *"the next day Moses took his seat to serve as judge for the people and they all stood around him from morning to night." 18:13*

Now, if 600,000 men + women and children + "many other people" left Egypt with Moses (12:37-38)....can you imagine how exhausting it must have been to hear complaints and arguments ALL DAY LONG!!

The Bible doesn't say how long Moses had been doing this when Jethro arrived. It's clear Jethro was able to assess the situation with clearer "lenses" than Moses. In today's slang Jethro asked, "Moses, are you out of your mind???"

I would imagine Moses thought he was fulfilling what God had called him to do. I also can't help but think Moses was starting to get a little tired of the calling he thought God had placed on his life.

When we try to be all things to everyone we not only rob ourselves of sanity and strength but rob those God has called to come alongside us in His service of their calling. By our actions we relay the message that "our" calling is more important than theirs.

Perhaps what we are trying to accomplish is not even to be accomplished, but we try anyway out of guilt (ours or others imposed on us), not wanting to let go of previous ways or possibly because we are trying to walk in another person's shoes that are not our size!

We will never be able to make everyone happy and we were never meant to do so. Again, we are stealing their reliance from God to us. That will never be a calling of God on anyone's life!

A true leader admits his limits and always points those he is leading to God.
"I am the Lord; that is my name! I will not give my glory to anyone else, nor share my praise with carved idols."
(Isaiah 42:8)

4. **We must be open to instruction...never stop learning—not be a know-it-all**. Exodus 18:17-26:

Moses could have copped an attitude with Jethro when he challenged him on his leadership skills. Instead he listened.

The first step to being open to instruction is to have an open mind, heart, and ear which requires us not to be thinking of excuses or indignation, "I KNOW what I'm doing...who do they think they are!"
A true leader will always have a hunger to learn more.

Jethro reminded Moses not to "spoon feed" but teach the people when he advised Moses to:
- Continue to represent the people before God
- Teach them God's decrees
- Instruct them
- Show they how to conduct their lives (don't try to conduct their lives for them)

Too often our importance is mistakenly wrapped up in others' dependence on us. We do them a great disservice in holding them hostage because of our insecurities and lack of trust.

"My child, listen to what I say and treasure my commands. Tune your ears to wisdom, and concentrate on understanding. Cry out for insight, and ask for understanding. For the Lord grants wisdom! From his

mouth come knowledge and understanding. He grants a treasure of common sense to the honest. He is a shield to those who walk with integrity. For wisdom will enter your heart, and knowledge will fill you with joy. Wise choices will watch over you. Understanding will keep you safe. My child, never forget the things I have taught you. Store my commands in your heart. Trust in the Lord with all your heart; do not depend on your own understanding. Seek his will in all you do, and he will show you which path to take. Don't be impressed with your own wisdom." (Proverbs 2-3 excerpts)

5. **Surround yourself with people who will support you** (Exodus 17:8-13).

   God never calls us to be "Lone Rangers."

   When we surround ourselves with only "I...me...myself" we fall prey to self-absorption, self-adulation, and exhaustion. When we allow others to get close to us, to see us in our highs and lows, we open the door to humility and close the door to pride.

   Not everyone will be a leader. Some are called to be a support. When a leader becomes vulnerable and admits he cannot do this on his own, he allows others to operate in the calling God has placed on their lives as a support. Both are important to the fulfilling of a calling. We need each other.

   Everyone (including leaders) is called to be a support and encouragement to others.

Who is your Aaron and Hur who will support, encourage, and pray for you in the calling God has placed on your life? Or for whom is God calling you to be an Aaron and Hur?

6. **Know the role you are to fill and release others to the roles they are to fill** (Exodus 17:8-9). God was already raising up Joshua to assume leadership. Moses had to begin to allow Joshua to walk in it.

Moses was called to lead, but Joshua's leading would look different because of where he would take the Israelites. Don't force your style or calling on the one who will come after you but be their support (Moses prayed while Joshua fought).

Elisha became a protégé to Elijah, learning the workings of a prophet by following, listening, and observing Elijah. Elisha knew he would have a ministry, but timing was everything...he would have to wait. Elijah would have to have patience and be willing to encourage and guide Elisha.

The calling God has me walking in is and will always be...His. 1 Corinthians 1:9: "God has called us to partner with him."

7. **Make sure we encourage the one who is to follow us in what God is calling him to do and encourage him in front of others** (Exodus 17:14-16).

Paul made very clear the source of his calling throughout the letters he wrote with proclamations such as, "This letter is from Paul, an *apostle* of Christ Jesus, *appointed by the command of God* our Savior and Christ Jesus." (1 Timothy 1:1 underline added)

He then cements the authority and calling in Timothy to lead the Ephesian church regardless of Timothy's age (1 Timothy 4:12).

Whether Paul, and the other New Testament writers, wrote to specific groups such as Corinth, Philippi, Ephesus, etc., the letters were to be read to the specific church and then sent on to other areas.

> *"After you have read this letter, pass it on to the church at the Laodicea so they can read it, too. And you should read the letter I wrote to them." (Colossians 4:16)*

In doing this, Paul was encouraging the leaders of each of those churches and confirming in everyone's minds the calling God placed upon each of those leaders.

Times were extremely difficult, persecutions were a daily threat, their lives were hanging by a thread...daily. Hearts and commitments to Jesus Christ were daily tested with some even denying Jesus Christ to avoid death. Many more faced death with a confident hope in the truth and promises of the Living God.

Paul encouraged Timothy, his son in the faith, to "cling to your faith" (1 Timothy 1:19); to "be an example to others in what you say and how you live" (1 Timothy 4:12); to "fan into flames the spiritual gift God gave you" (2 Timothy 1); to "hold onto the truth" (2 Timothy 1:13); etc.

We don't find anywhere in scripture where Paul told Timothy he had to lead the exact same way Paul led. Paul does say to "imitate him" but only in the faith and walk Paul has led in following Jesus Christ, always pointing others to Jesus and not himself.

8. **Our calling is not a popularity contest.**
    - Know who and whose you are (2 Corinthians 3:5).
    - Cautiously accept what another prays or prophesy over you and ministry "advice" from others. Prophecy must be tested against scripture. There are false prophets just as charismatic or genuine sounding as God-sent prophets. (1 Thessalonians 5:19-21).
    - Don't base the "success" of your calling on the acceptance or agreement of others. Some have believed and based their calling on the accolades of others over the power and movement of God in their lives. Success in our abilities will be short

lived. Success through God's abilities will be eternally lived.

- God's calling and gifts are not cookie cutter, one-size-fits-all. He uses our individual personalities, so don't try to mimic another.
- "Examine yourselves to see if your faith is genuine. Test yourselves." (2 Corinthians 13:5)
- Pray without ceasing. Prayer keeps our focus on God not a popular opinion. (Ephesians 6:18)

"So we keep on praying for you, asking our God to enable you to live a life worthy of his call. May he give you the power to accomplish all the good things your faith prompts you to do."
2 Thessalonians 1:11

"Since, then, we know what it is to fear the Lord, we try to persuade others. What we are is plain to God, and I hope it is also plain to your conscience. We are not trying to commend ourselves to you again, but are giving you an opportunity to take pride in us, so that you can answer those who take pride in what is seen rather than in what is in the heart. If we are 'out of our mind,' as some say, it is for God; if we are in our right mind, it is for you. For Christ's love compels us, because we are convinced that one died for all, and therefore all died. And he died for all, that those who live should no longer live for themselves but for him who died for them and was raised again. So from now on we regard no one from a worldly point of view. Though we once regarded Christ in this way, we do so no longer. Therefore, if anyone is in Christ, the

new creation has come: The old has gone, the new is here! All this is from God, who reconciled us to himself through Christ and gave us the ministry of reconciliation: that God was reconciling the world to himself in Christ, not counting people's sins against them. And he has committed to us the message of reconciliation. We are therefore Christ's ambassadors, as though God were making his appeal through us. We implore you on Christ's behalf: Be reconciled to God. God made him who had no sin to be sin for us, so that in him we might become the righteousness of God." (2 Corinthians 5:11-21 NIV)

HOMEWORK = link between what we have <u>learned</u> and what we <u>think</u> about, which results in what we put into <u>practice</u>

Which of the eight lessons listed above speaks to you and why?

Whom do you surround to support in their calling?

Who surrounds you in your calling?

Have you ever felt burned out in your calling because you had to "be everything" or "do everything?"

Is it hard for you to allow or accept others' help? Ask the Lord to examine your heart. Then be obedient and act upon what He is showing you.

Psalm 119:29

Psalm 139:23-24

Chapter Six
Obedience is the Best Travel Companion...Exodus 23

Teach me your way, O Lord, and I will walk in your truth; give me an undivided heart, that I may fear your name. I will praise you, O Lord my God, with all my heart; I will glorify your name forever.
Psalm 86:11-12 (NIV)
Teach me your decrees, O Lord, I will keep them to the end. Give me understanding and I will obey your instructions; I will put them into practice with all my heart. Make me walk along the path of your commands, for that is where my happiness is found.
Psalm 119:33-35

Aren't we there yet??

When I was about 12 years old my mom and her best friend loaded us five kids into a station wagon and headed for a visit with my grandparents in Florida. We would cheer every time we passed a sign that announced our entry into a new state. We passed a sign that said, "Welcome to West Virginia" and began cheering, only to have my mom say, "We're not supposed to go through West Virginia!" Good thing there was a sign to let us know we were on the wrong road.

Lori M

Over the years my one aunt had acquired multiple timeshares throughout the East Coast. Prior to her marriage, she would occasionally invite me to travel with her. Since she drove to most of the locations, she always kept a travel box with dish soap, paper towels, garbage bags, matches, etc. in the trunk of her car.

The box I keep in my car consists of paper towels, disinfectant wipes, first aid kit, and a sweater and sweatshirt. When we travel I throw a blanket and travel pillows in it too.

What are the staples with which you travel?

Years ago, before GPS was available, we would always get TripTiks from AAA before traveling. They were better than state maps because more details along the route were given. As long as we followed the routes they picked for us, we had no problem getting to our destination, barring any traffic delays or detours.

Today's GPS is a hundred times better than the TripTiks because the directions are in real time, and if I take a wrong turn, that lovely voice lets me know it and gets me back on track!

For the Israelites, no TripTiks or GPS could ever have outweighed the ultimate direction and leading of God in their journey to the Promised Land! And just like our current GPS announces "recalculating" when we take a wrong turn, God had to recalculate their hearts back on track to obedience to His direction many times.

I am so very thankful God gave us His Holy Spirit to be our GPS today (we could rename it to "**G**od's **P**rotective **S**ervice")! As with the Israelites, there are many times He has had to recalculate my heart back on track to His leading and direction for my life.

Jesus said in John 14:15-21

"If you love me, obey my commandments. And I will ask the Father, and he will give you another Advocate, who will never leave you. He is the Holy Spirit, who leads into all truth. The world cannot receive him, because it isn't looking for him and doesn't recognize him. But you know him, because he lives with you now and later will be in you. No, I will not abandon you as orphans – I will come to you...Those who accept my commandments and obey them are the ones who love me. And because they love me, my Father will love them. And I will love them and reveal myself to each of them."

Love and obedience go hand-in-hand. Obedience without love is short-lived and easily persuaded and manipulated. Love without obedience is shallow and emotionally driven.

To love AND obey means we trust and feel safe in whom we love knowing they would never do or ask us to do anything that would compromise their integrity or ours.

Clearly God had proven His love, His integrity, His power, His ability to deliver, provide, and protect the Israelites from the moment they stepped out of their bondage in Egypt. Why would

He change any of that now? Yet throughout their journey God had to remind the Israelites of His expectations of obedience and the consequences of not fulfilling them.

God has not changed in His expectations of obedience from us today.

Let's see what we can unpack in Exodus chapter 23 that can help us in our walk of obedient love.

Exodus 23:20-22; Deuteronomy 6-11

1. **God goes before us to lead us along the way**

   In John 10 Jesus compares Himself to a shepherd leading his flock:

   > "*The gatekeeper opens the gate for him and the sheep recognize his voice and come to him. He calls his own sheep by name and leads them out. After he has gathered his own flock, he walks ahead of them, and they follow him because they know his voice. They won't follow a stranger; they will run from him because they don't know his voice.*" *(John 10:3-5)*

   Shepherds commonly shared a sheepfold with other shepherds and their flocks. This was a protective place where both sheep and shepherds could rest during the night knowing their flocks were safe. In the morning the shepherds asked the gatekeeper to open the gate. They would call their sheep, and only the sheep of that particular shepherd would go to him because the sheep knew and trusted his voice.

We may never actually hear the audible voice of God today, but we have His Word and His Holy Spirit living within us that He promised would speak Truth to us.

> *"If you love me, obey my commandments. And I will ask the Father, and he will give you another Advocate, who will never leave you. He is the Holy Spirit, who leads into all truth...Those who accept my commandments and obey them are the ones who love me. And because they love me, my Father will love them. And I will love them and reveal myself to each of them...All who love me will do what I say. My Father will love them, and we will come and make our home with each of them...But when the father sends the Advocate as my representative – that is, the Holy Spirit – he will teach you everything and remind you of everything I have told you.... When the Spirit of truth comes, he will guide you into all truth. He will not speak on his own but will tell you what he has heard..." (John 14:15-17, 21,23, 26; 16:13)*

God will never lead us astray from His path, His Truth. He knows all and has seen all. He knew our beginning in this life, He knows our end, and He knows the in-between. We know our past and only the very second we call "now."

Only when we listen for...wait for...and hear the voice of our shepherd, Jesus, should we move forward in our journey knowing He will never lead us on a path of lies or deceit. If what you are hearing is contrary to His truths, stand firm until you hear God's voice!

2. **Obedience allows us to take possession of our territory from the enemy.**

Obedience is not a physical object we can touch. It is a decision formulated first in our minds then revealed through our actions.

Today, you and I don't conquer physical enemies to enter our Promised Land but spiritual enemies. Yes, sometimes those enemies manifest themselves through others, but the truth remains their origins are of a spiritual nature. We can't fight spiritual battles with physical weapons.
Paul tells us:

> "The weapons we fight with are not the weapons of the world. On the contrary, **they have divine power to demolish strongholds**. We demolish arguments and every pretension that sets itself up against the knowledge of God, and we take captive every thought to make it obedient to Christ." (2 Corinthians 10:4-5 NIV bold added)

The NLT version:

> "We are human, but we don't wage war as humans do. We use God's mighty weapons, not worldly weapons, to knock down the strongholds of human

reasoning and to destroy false arguments." (2 Corinthians 10:3-4)

Human reasoning and false arguments (based on human reasoning) are strongholds and the very place most of our spiritual battlefields find us.

Some of our "territories" may be our marriages, wayward children, substance abuse, fear, disappointment, bitterness, unforgiveness, etc.

James tells us we need patience, staying power, endurance, never giving up, refusing to surrender as part of our spiritual arsenal (James 1).

Paul tells us:

> *"...Be strong in the Lord and in his mighty power. Put on all of God's armor so that you will be able to stand firm against all strategies of the devil. For we are not fighting against flesh-and-blood enemies, but against evil rulers and authorities of the unseen world, against mighty powers in this dark world, and against evil spirits in the heavenly places. Therefore, put on every piece of God's armor so you will be able to resist the enemy in the time of evil. Then after the battle you will still be standing firm. Stand your ground, putting on the belt of truth and the body armor of God's righteousness. For shoes, put on the peace that comes from the Good News so that you will be fully prepared. In addition*

*to all of these, hold up the shield of faith to stop the
fiery arrows of the devil. Put on salvation as your
helmet, and take the sword of the Spirit, which is
the word of God. Pray in the Spirit at all times and
on every occasion. Stay alert and be persistent in
your prayers for all believers everywhere."
(Ephesians 6:10-18 underline added)*

Obedience does not give up no matter what comes
against us but "stands firm" because of Whom we are
obeying and trusting.

Again, this is not a physical place but rather a spiritual
battle that must be fought with spiritual weapons. It must
be fought in His power and by His power, fought with
weapons that have divine power because they are backed
by and infused with the power of God.

Moses' faith in God to deliver the Israelites from the
Egyptians when their backs were against the sea was one
of the weapons Paul said had "divine power to demolish
strongholds." Their stronghold was the Egyptian army, and
it was demolished that day!
Moses stood firm in his faith, and Israel took possession of
their territory because God fought for them with divine
weapons.
We will be able to take possession of the territories God
promises us; take back what the enemy has stolen from us
(John 10:10) in marriages, wayward children, sound

minds rather than fearful minds, etc. when we remain obedient and stand firm on His promises. We have His divine power to demolish our strongholds.

3. **Our obedience looks different from what the world defines obedience.**

> *"Don't copy the behavior and customs of this world, but let God transform you into a new person by changing the way you think. Then you will learn to know God's will for you, which is good and pleasing and perfect." (Romans 12:2)*

The world's view of obedience is only if it is convenient or profitable for you. The world's view is all about "me."

Obedience comes with a cost.
Obedience requires denial of self.
Obedience requires sacrifice.
Obedience can be messy.
Obedience requires abiding, remaining...not running or giving up.
Obedience requires surrender and submitting.
Obedience may require suffering.
Obedience doesn't always give a reason.

4. **God establishes our borders...boundaries. Be careful to stay within them, to obey.**
We tend to look at words like "boundaries," "surrender," and "submission" negatively and sense a loss of freedom.

The reality is there are borders and boundaries in everything and all around us. By their very nature, the lack or absence of them would actually mean no freedom and chaos.

Galatians chapters 5 and 6 describe chaos without these spiritual borders which bleed over to our physical and emotional borders:

> "So Christ has truly set us free. Now make sure that you stay free, and don't get tied up again in slavery to the law.
> For you have been called to live in freedom, my brothers and sisters. But don't use your freedom to satisfy your sinful nature. Instead, use your freedom to serve one another in love.
> So I say, let the Holy Spirit guide your lives. Then you won't be doing what your sinful nature craves. The sinful nature wants to do evil, which is just the opposite of what the Spirit wants. And the Spirit gives us desires that are the opposite of what the sinful nature desires. These two forces are constantly fighting each other, so you are not free to carry out your good intentions.
> When you follow the desires of your sinful nature, the results are very clear: sexual immorality, impurity, lustful pleasures, idolatry, sorcery, hostility, quarreling, jealousy, outbursts of anger, selfish ambition, dissension, division, envy, drunkenness, wild parties, and other sins like

these. Let me tell you again, as I have before, that anyone living that sort of life will not inherit the Kingdom of God.

But the Holy Spirit produces this kind of fruit in our lives: love, joy, peace, patience, kindness, goodness, faithfulness, gentleness, and self-control. There is no law against these things! Those who belong to Christ Jesus have nailed the passions and desires of their sinful nature to his cross and crucified them there. Since we are living by the Spirit, let us follow the Spirit's leading in every part of our lives. Let us not become conceited, or provoke one another, or be jealous of one another." (Galatians 5:1, 13, 16-17, 19-26)

"Don't be misled—you cannot mock the justice of God. You will always harvest what you plant. Those who live only to satisfy their own sinful nature will harvest decay and death from that sinful nature. But those who live to please the Spirit will harvest everlasting life from the Spirit." (Galatians 6:7-8)

In fact Paul describes life without God's borders as slavery in Romans chapters 6-8. Slavery is the opposite of freedom! Our obedience to God and His ways, His divine boundaries, ensures a life of freedom, not slavery, but we must remain within those boundaries to receive His blessings.

Boundaries are not about exclusivity but reward, hope, life, freedom, and safety to anyone willing to sacrifice his own path for one that is better.

5. **Obedience out of fear never sustains us when troubles come.**
   Exodus 20:18-20; 24:3-8
   Tyrants and dictators demand obedience to their rule, or imprisonment, torture, and/or death awaits. Fear is the basis of their subjects' obedience.

   If obedience is given out of fear rather than love we will be looking for the closest Exit Sign from the relationship when troubles come. The commitment to stay will be dust in the wind as we leave Dodge!! Peter looked for this "Exit Sign" in his denial of Jesus in the courtyard when Jesus was being questioned the night of His arrest. At the first sign of trouble, denial was the result of Peter's shallow promise to obey (*"I'm ready to die for you." John 13:37*)

   It wasn't until AFTER Jesus death and resurrection the disciples understood the "if you love me you will obey" teachings of Jesus. They understood love requires obedience, and obedience is built on love. They understood the One Who required true unadulterated obedience was also the One they could trust with their very lives in what He was asking them to obey.

6. **Just as there are blessings of obedience there are also punishments (consequences) of disobedience.** We must never be in such a hurry to pledge our obedience without fully comprehending the consequences of our disobedience.

Time after time the people pledged their obedience to do all the Lord was requiring of them when Moses revealed God's Word/instructions to them. And time after time the people suffered the consequences of their disobedience because their obedience was short lived. God would remind the Israelites of these blessings and curses multiple times throughout Leviticus and Deuteronomy.

The blessings far outweighed the punishment, yet the people constantly chose, by their actions, disobedience and the consequences.

Blessings of obedience (Leviticus 26:3-13)

> *"If you follow my decrees and are careful to obey my commands..."*

God will send the seasonal rains. The land will yield its crops and trees their fruit. They will eat their fill and live securely in their land. They will have a surplus of crops so they will have to clear out the previous year's grain to make room for the new harvest.

God will give them peace in the land, and they will be able to sleep with no fear. He will rid the land of wild animals and will keep their enemies out of their land. In fact, they will chase down their enemies, and they will fall beneath their swords.

God will make them fertile so the people will multiply.

God will fulfill His covenant with them.

God will live among them, and He will not despise them.

God will walk among them.

God will be their God, and they will be His people.

They will be God's own special treasure from among all the peoples of the earth (Exodus 19:5).

Punishments for disobedience (Leviticus 26:14-39)

> *"However, if you do not listen to me or obey all these commands, and if you break my covenant by rejecting my decrees, treating my regulations with contempt, and refusing to obey my commands, I will punish you."*

God will bring sudden terror among them. They will be afflicted with wasting diseases and failing eyes, and their lives will ebb away. Their crops will be eaten by their enemies. Rain will be withheld, as the earth will be as hard as bronze. They will work in vain...no harvest will be had. Disaster will be inflicted upon them; wild animals will rob them of their children and livestock. Armies will overtake them; famine will overtake them.

They will turn to useless pagan worship even eating the flesh of their own sons and daughters. They will be scattered among the nations, their land desolate and their cities ruined.

And the list goes on......

Blessings or punishments really come down to one word...choice. We choose whether we will obey or disobey. Throughout the New Testament God once again gives blessings of obedience and consequences of disobedience. And like the Israelites, we can choose to obey or disobey; we choose blessings or punishments.

I love the encouragement God gave the Israelites and one we can hold onto today:

> *"This command I am giving you today is not too difficult for you to understand, and it is not beyond your reach...Today I have given you the choice between life and death, between blessings and curses...Now I call on heaven and earth to witness the choice you make. Oh, that you would choose life, so that you and your descendants might live! You can make this choice by loving the Lord your God, obeying him, and committing yourself firmly to him. This is the key to your life." Deuteronomy 30:11-20*

7. **Effects of repentance-returning to obedience**

Unfortunately the yo-yo of obedience and disobedience was the Israelites' path from the time they left Egypt to the entrance of the Promised Land and beyond. Their history was peppered with blessings and punishments throughout the Old Testament.

But through it all, God never forsook nor forgot His covenant, His oath, and His promises to Abraham, Isaac, and Jacob.

""But at last my people will confess their sins and the sins of their ancestors for betraying me and being hostile toward me. When I have turned their hostility back on them and brought them to the land of their enemies, then at last their stubborn hearts will be humbled, and they will pay for their sins. Then I will remember my covenant with Jacob and my covenant with Isaac and my covenant with Abraham, and I will remember the land.
"But despite all this, I will not utterly reject or despise them while they are in exile in the land of their enemies. I will not cancel my covenant with them by wiping them out, for I am the Lord their God. For their sakes I will remember my ancient covenant with their ancestors, whom I brought out of the land of Egypt in the sight of all the nations, that I might be their God. I am the Lord.""(Leviticus 26:40-42, 44-45)

"I will certainly bring my people back again from all the countries where I will scatter them in my fury. I will bring them back to this very city and let them live in peace and safety...And I will give them one heart and one purpose: to worship me forever, for their own good and for the good of all their descendants. And I will make an everlasting

covenant with them: I will never stop doing good for them. I will put a desire in their hearts to worship me, and they will never leave me. I will find joy doing good for them and will faithfully and wholeheartedly replant them in this land. "This is what the Lord says: Just as I have brought all these calamities on them, so I will do all the good I have promised them." (Jeremiah 32:37, 39-42)

Likewise today God longs for us, waits for us to return from our disobedience to repentance so He can restore life, hope, and peace in our hearts and minds.

"For the kind of sorrow God wants us to experience leads us away from sin and results in salvation. There's no regret for that kind of sorrow. But worldly sorrow, which lacks repentance, results in spiritual death." (2 Corinthians 7:10)

"Therefore, since we have been made right in God's sight by faith, we have peace with God because of what Jesus Christ our Lord has done for us. Because of our faith, Christ has brought us into this place of undeserved privilege where we now stand, and we confidently and joyfully look forward to sharing God's glory...When we were utterly helpless, Christ came at just the right time and died for us sinners...But God showed his great love for us by sending Christ to die for us while we were still sinners. And since we have been made

right in God's sight by the blood of Christ, he will
certainly save us from God's condemnation. For
since our friendship with God was restored by the
death of his Son while we were still his enemies,
we will certainly be saved through the life of his
Son. So now we can rejoice in our wonderful new
relationship with God because our Lord Jesus
Christ has made us friends of God." (Romans 5:1-
2, 6, 8-11)

When our son was in middle school, his classroom had a
pet snake. Prior to Christmas break the teacher asked if someone
would be willing to take the snake home to care for it over break.

Our son asked me if he was allowed to bring the snake
home. "Absolutely not, I do not want a snake in this house!" was
my response. Christmas break arrived, and our daughter had a
friend over for a sleepover. We awoke in the morning to screams
from the girls. When I raced downstairs to see what the problem
was, there was a snake lying on the step! I opened the front door
and brushed the snake outside. I believe he was glad to get away
from the screams! Our son happened to be at a friend's house for
a sleepover that night and didn't realize we had discovered the
snake and his disobedience.

At the beginning of school that year we had moved, and
our son still had boxes piled in his room that I had been after him
to clean out and put his things away. I told the girls not to say
anything to him when he got home that day from his friend's

house. When he came home he went straight to his room and started going through boxes. After waiting a while, I went in and told him how proud I was that he was finally accomplishing the task he had been told to do months before and then I said, "it almost looks like you are searching for something. Could it be you're looking for...a snake?" His eyes became as big as saucers, and I told him the snake had been found and delivered to the outside where it belonged. We laid on his bed talked about disobedience and had a good laugh at the end result of his finally being obedient in cleaning out his boxes!

HOMEWORK = link between what we have <u>learned</u> and what we <u>think</u> about, which results in what we put into <u>practice</u>

Where in your faith walk have you struggled with obedience?

Read John 8:30-31 Believing is not the same as remaining, why?

What are the promises of remaining in John 15:1-17?

John 14:15-31 If we _____ Him we will _____ Him and _____ His commandments

Who is promised to reside in us?

What gift does Jesus give?

Who was obedient, and what did His obedience cost and for whom?

Chapter Seven
Service...Gift or Burden? Numbers 18

And may the Lord our God show us his approval and make our
efforts successful. Yes, make our efforts successful!
Psalm 90:17

Aren't we there yet??

My parents were taking me to college. We had my
grandpa's Taurus loaded down with all my stuff. My brother
and I squished into one seat in the backseat. My mom heard
someone say, "stop biting my foot!!" and the other one say,
"then stop putting your foot in my mouth!!"

I'm pretty sure I was the one biting because his foot
was in my face! Lol..it was a very tight squeeze..

Bethany N

We begin this chapter with an interesting story in Numbers
16:1-16 that I'm sure anyone who has been in ministry can relate
to:

"One day Korah, a descendent of Levi, conspired with Dathan
and Abiram...they incited a rebellion against Moses... 'You have
gone too far!...what right do you have to act as though you are
greater than the rest of the Lord's people?'

When Moses heard what they were saying, he fell face down
on the ground.

'Now listen, you Levites! Does it seem insignificant to you that the God of Israel has chosen you from among all the community of Israel to be near him so you can serve in the Lord's tabernacle and stand before the people to minister to them? Korah, he has already given this special ministry to you and your fellow Levites. Are you now demanding the priesthood as well? The Lord is the one you and your followers are really revolting against! For who is Aaron that you are complaining about him?'

The story continues to reveal Korah stirred up the whole community against Moses and Aaron, and once again Moses found himself face down, pleading with God not to destroy this nation *"when only one man has sinned." (Numbers 16:22)*
God instructs Moses to get all the people away from the tents of Korah, Dathan, and Abiram. When all the people moved away, *"...the ground suddenly split open and swallowed the men along with their households (wives, children and little ones), everything they owned, and anyone standing with them. So they went down alive into the grave, along with all their belongings. The earth closed over them, and they all vanished from among the people of Israel." (Numbers 16:31-33)*

What happened to these men and their families sounds pretty drastic! But if we are honest, there may have been times when we wished our adversaries would just "go away."

If it weren't for dealing with people, ministry/service would be an amazing experience! If we could just do "our thing" then go home, lock the door behind us, and bar the naysayers...yep, ministry would be amazing!!

A heart filled with jealousy and self-promotion will never be a heart pliable for God to mold and use in His service. Korah's jealousy was not a God-inspired jealousy that longs for the things of God, to direct man's attention and a love focused on God. His was a self-jealousy that longs for attention and adoration from mankind to mankind.

SERVICE IS A GIFT

"I myself have chosen your fellow Levites from among the Israelites to be your special assistants. They are a gift to you, dedicated to the Lord for service in the Tabernacle...I am giving you the priesthood as your special privilege of service..." Numbers 18:6-7

Do we consider *service* as a gift, or do we consider *ourselves* as the gift to service?
Our mindset (heart set) determines our focus, which determines our availability for God to mold or remold us for use in *His* service.

If we enter into a time of service/ministry thinking about what we can offer or bring "to the table," it will always be about fitting our agenda into the opportunities set before us. Clearly Korah's heart was inward focused on whatever his agenda was.

Service/ministry is about teamwork. God specifically chose Aaron and his sons, from the tribe of Levi, to makeup the priesthood. The remaining relatives from Levi were to serve as their assistants in the different duties regarding the Tabernacle. Notice God said, *"your fellow Levites are a gift to you, dedicated to the Lord for service in the Tabernacle."*

First and foremost they were dedicated to the Lord for the Lord's service, not Aaron's. Secondly they were a gift to Aaron (and his descendants) as helpers in the work God ordained for the priesthood. When we are part of a team we are first a gift to serve God together, then a gift to serve each other together. We are dedicated individually to and for God's service, THEN to and for service with each other.

The big question is, do we look at our service with and to others, as a gift or a burden? When others' gifting doesn't line up with our expectations, do we still believe they are a gift or burden to "our" ministry/service? As leaders, is it easier to dismiss them or take the time to encourage and guide them?

GOD EQUIPS US FOR HIS SERVICE

In Exodus chapters 35-36 we read the Lord specifically chose certain men and *"filled them with the Spirit of God, giving them great wisdom, ability, and expertise in all kinds of crafts...and the ability to teach their skills to others."* (35:30-34)

Just as God equipped the Israelites in the infancy days of their nation to works of service to Him, He equips us today in service to Him. The same Spirit of God Who enabled them, enables us today, living in us as a constant partner in our service!

"Now may the God of peace...equip you with all you need for doing his will. May he produce in you, through the power of Jesus Christ, every good thing that is pleasing to him. All glory to Him forever and ever! Amen." (Hebrews 13:20-21)

Paul begins 1 Corinthians 12 with the reminder that while there are different spiritual gifts, the Holy Spirit is the Source of them all, and while there are different kinds of service, it is God who does the work, is the Source, in all of us.

This is a great reminder when "self" tends to get in the way of our service. No one is better or greater than another in his gifts or service because ultimately "we" are not the Source...only the Source is great and praise worthy!

Paul then instructs, *"A spiritual gift is given to each of us so we can help each other." (12:7)*

1 Corinthians chapters 12 and 14 list some of the gifts the Spirit gives. 1 Corinthians 12:11 reminds us, *"It is the one and only Spirit who distributes all these gifts. He alone decides which gift each person should have."* And just as God decides which gift we are to have, He also decides where in the body of Christ He wants that gift to fit (12:18).

God will place some people with their gifts in a very visible arena, while others, maybe even with the same gifts, will be used in "behind-the-scenes" arenas...both powerfully used by God. Paul encourages his readers to *"earnestly desire the most helpful gifts" (12:31).* Notice he doesn't say most visible, most recognizable, or most powerful in our eyes.

Sandwiched between the description of the gifts, in chapters 12 and 14, is a detour about love in chapter 13...or is a detour?

Human nature can get a little sticky when it comes to self-denial and giving of ourselves for the good of others without being acknowledged or rewarded. Paul reminds us that we can have the most "successful," the most "coveted," gifts, but if we are operating in them for anything other than serving God and giving God the glory, they will be to others like a "noisy, offensive 'off cue' clanging of a cymbal."

I have witnessed some who clearly have been given certain gifts to then use them as springboards for their own advantage. And still others have not used grace in operating in their gifts and as a result have destroyed those whom they could have helped had they waited for God's timing and His "grace-peppered" words to speak correction and truth.

Paul's discourse on love (1 Corinthians 13) and its position in the scriptures provides the "meat in the sandwich" of gifts. Love is the meat, the flavor that permeates the gifts that strengthen, encourage, and comfort the body of Christ. A word of correction or truth wrapped in love can be the very avenue by which the Holy Spirit is welcomed by the recipient to do the work only He can do in transforming or tenderizing a heart.

Aaron's sons abused their gift of the priesthood in Leviticus 10. Throughout scripture we read there were obedient, righteous priests and disobedient, unrighteous priests. There will always be counterfeit and abuse with any good gift God gives, but don't let others' abuse prevent you from living out the purpose God has for you and the gifts He has given you to enable you to live in His service. Let us, like David, pray:

"Search me, O God, and know my heart; test me and know my anxious thoughts. Point out anything in me that offends you, and lead me along the path of everlasting life." (Psalms 139:23-24)

I believe pride and false humility are the biggest stumbling blocks of our obedience and operating in spiritual gifts.

Paul tells us in Ephesians chapter 4 the gifts Christ gave to the church are to be used to equip, build up, and encourage unity in our faith and knowledge of Jesus Christ. Sometimes in the building up and encouraging we can get lost in the focus of the gifts. We focus too much on the gifts rather than the Giver of those gifts. If we aren't careful, this is where pride and false humility comes into play.

"...Are your hearts tender and compassionate? Then make me truly happy by agreeing wholeheartedly with each other, loving one another, and working together with one mind and purpose. Don't be selfish; don't try to impress others. Be humble, thinking of others as better than yourselves. Don't look out for your own interest, but take an interest in others, too." (Philippians 2:1-4)

May I suggest we encourage each other, focusing the attention on the Source of the gift and not the vehicle. For example:

- "I thank God for you and how the Lord is using you in/with_____."

   Instead of, "You are awesome...amazing!"

- "I know it hasn't been easy to stand firm in _____, but God is working in you and He will give you the power to_____."

   Instead of, "Who do they think they are! Don't they know you_____?"

We live in a world that rewards job performance in the individual. Sometimes that standard and recognition bleeds over into our spiritual works.

"Work willingly at whatever you do, as though you were working for the Lord rather than for people. Remember that the Lord will give you an inheritance as your reward, and that the Master you are serving is Christ." (Colossians 3:23-24)

God gives the gift for His purposes and for His glory.

"God has united you with Christ Jesus. For our benefit God made him to be wisdom itself. Christ made us right with God; he made us pure and holy, and he freed us from sin. Therefore, as the Scriptures say, 'if you want to boast, boast only about the Lord'." (1 Corinthians 1:30-31)

SUFFERING IS ALSO PART OF SERVICE

"For you have been given not only the privilege of trusting in Christ but also the privilege of suffering for him." (Philippians 1:29)

In our Western Christian culture, we have yet to truly experience the suffering and persecution our brothers and sisters have and are experiencing in other parts of the world.

Recently, lawsuits have been filed against businesses because they have chosen not to cater to those who would compromise their faith-beliefs. I'm not suggesting these individuals, their businesses, and their families have not suffered financially, emotionally, and for some even physical death threats. But for the most part, as a Christian in the United States, we can still work, shop, live, and enjoy recreational freedoms without fear of illegal imprisonment or government mandated deaths all because of our faith...so far!

Jesus was very clear that to be His follower, we would experience the same hatred of the world He experienced.

"If the world hates you, keep in mind that it hated me first. If you belonged to the world, it would love you as its own. As it is, you do not belong to the world, but I have chosen you out of the world. That is why the world hates you. Remember what I told you: 'A servant is not greater than his master.' If they persecuted me, they will persecute you also. If they obeyed my teaching, they will obey yours also.

They will treat you this way because of my name, for they do not know the one who sent me." (John 15:18-21 NIV)

"All this I have told you so that you will not fall away. They will put you out of the synagogue; in fact, the time is coming when anyone who kills you will think they are offering a service to God. They will do such things because they have not known the Father or me. I have told you this, so that when their time comes you will remember that I warned you about them." (John 16:1-4 NIV)

Suffering is part of obedience. I'm not referring to false suffering due to our foolishness. We probably all know the story of someone or an organization that cried "persecution" when in reality it was their own foolishness that caused their troubles.

Jesus walked this very path of suffering in obedience to His Father. Jesus left the grandeur and magnificence of heaven, the adoration and worship from the angels, and the intimacy and oneness with the Father to take on the humble robe of servanthood called humanity. He came to a world that neither understood His mission nor acknowledged its need of His mission. He came to a selfish and self-serving world to serve, not to be served. He came to suffer at the hands of those whom He was intimately involved in creating. He came to teach us many things, one of which was suffering.

"In the days of His earthly life, Jesus offered up both [specific] petitions and [urgent] supplications [for that which He needed] with fervent crying and tears to the One

who was [always] able to save Him from death, and He was heard because of His reverent submission toward God [His sinlessness and His unfailing determination to do the Father's will]. Although He was a Son [who had never been disobedient to the Father], He learned [active, special] obedience through what He suffered." (Hebrews 5:7-8 AMP)

The apostle Paul, writing from the horrendous conditions of a prison, reminded the Philippian believers to have the same attitude of Christ: humility of heart and mind, obedience in living unselfishly, and sacrificial love of others (Philippians 2:5-8). They were to have this attitude without complaining or arguing (Philippians 2:14). *"For you have been given not only the privilege of trusting in Christ but also the* <u>privilege of suffering for him</u>.*"* (Philippians 1:29 underline added)

The privilege of suffering!

Paul boldly proclaimed, *"I want to know Christ and experience the mighty power that raised him from the dead. I want to suffer with him, sharing in his death, so that one way or another I will experience the resurrection from the dead!"* (Philippians 3:10-11).

When Jesus called Saul (Paul) on his way to Damascus and struck him blind, He sent Ananias to lay hands on him so he could get his sight back. The Lord said to Ananias, *"Go, for Saul is my chosen instrument to take my message to the Gentiles and to kings, as well as to the people of Israel. And I will show him how much he must suffer for my name's sake."* (Acts 9:15)

Suffering was the very building block of Saul's calling, his service.

Suffering should not come as a surprise for the followers of Jesus Christ because the faith we are commanded, and committed to walk, is in direct opposition to what the world view and culture promotes. We're even given an example to follow for our conduct in suffering:

> *"For [as a believer] you have been called for this purpose, since Christ suffered for you, leaving you an example, so that you may follow in His footsteps. He committed no sin, nor was deceit ever found in his mouth. While being reviled and insulted, He did not revile or insult in return; while suffering, He made no threats [of vengeance], but kept entrusting Himself to Him who judges fairly."* (1 Peter 2:21-23 AMP)

> *"Who is going to harm you if you are eager to do good? But even if you should suffer for what is right, you are blessed. Do not fear their threats; do not be frightened. But in your hearts revere Christ as Lord. Always be prepared to give an answer to everyone who asks you to give the reason for the hope that you have. But do this with gentleness and respect, keeping a clear conscience, so that those who speak maliciously against your good behavior in Christ may be ashamed of their slander. For it is better, if it is God's will, to suffer for doing good than for doing evil."* (1 Peter 3:13-17 NIV)

Suffering is contrary to comfort. Paul and Barnabas encouraged the believers *"to continue in the faith, reminding them that we must suffer many hardships to enter the Kingdom of God."* (Acts 14:22)

Acts 5:41-42 tells us after the apostles were flogged they left the high council *"rejoicing that God counted them worthy to suffer disgrace for the name of Jesus...and they continued to teach and preach 'Jesus is the Messiah'."*

The following is from a recent edition of the monthly newsletter from "The Voice of The Martyrs":

> Many Sudanese believers have endured persecution for decades. One such believer was a pastor who was interrogated, beaten, and tortured during his second imprisonment lasting eight years in the 1980's. His persecutors tried to force him to reject Jesus, pulling out his fingernails, whipping him with wires and applying excruciating electrical shocks, but God helped the pastor endure the torture. "God showed me, 'I am with you.' God reminded me that the body can die but the soul cannot. Once I said to my torturers, 'you can torture me, but if you kill me I will just see Jesus!"[12]

---

[12] The Voice of the Martyrs/ Special Report "Sudan in Turmoil: What It Means for Christians, 05/2019

Signs and wonders are found in the midst of suffering and persecution (Acts 14:1-22); our faith can flourish in the midst of persecution (2 Thessalonians 1:3-7); and His strength is found in the midst of our weaknesses (2 Corinthians 12:7-10).

> *"...Christ is the power of God and the wisdom of God. This foolish plan of God is wiser than the wisest of human plans, and God's weakness is stronger than the greatest of human strength." (1 Corinthians 1:24-25)*

If suffering is what ushers in the miraculous moving power of God, would we then be willing to say, "Come Lord Jesus in all your power, that you might be glorified...that in my weakness (suffering) your strength would be seen?" If need be, would you and I be willing to suffer so others would come to know Jesus as Savior and Lord?

Will we be able to say as Paul, "the *privilege* of suffering" when we are put to the test?

Our service to God...is it a gift or a burden?

HOMEWORK = link between what we have <u>learned</u> and what we <u>think</u> about, which results in what we put into <u>practice</u>

List the spiritual gifts in each of these scripture references.
Romans 12

1 Peter 4:7-11

Ephesians 4:7-16

Colossians 3:12-17

Romans 15:2

Romans 14:12-23

1 Corinthians 12

What are the heart warnings in these verses?
2 Corinthians 10:12, 17-18

2 Corinthians 13:5

Romans 2:29

What do these verses have to say about suffering? What does that speak to you?
Acts 9:15-16

Romans 8:31-39

2 Timothy 2:3; 4:2-5

2 Timothy 1:6-12; 3:10-15

Chapter Eight
Stronghold of Fear...Numbers 13; Deuteronomy 1

I prayed to the Lord, and he answered me.
He freed me from all my fears.
Those who look to him for help will be radiant with joy;
no shadow of shame will darken their faces.
In my desperation I prayed, and the Lord listened;
he saved me from all my troubles. For the angel of the Lord is a
guard; he surrounds and defends all fear him.
Taste and see that the Lord is good.
Oh, the joys of those who take refuge in him!
Psalm 34:4-8

Aren't we there yet??

While my husband and I were in Clearwater, Florida, he wanted to jet ski, but I decided to stay at the beach. Later I went up to our room and opened the door to the balcony. It closed shut on me and locked. I was stuck on that balcony for three hours in full sun and with no water. Finally someone in the room next to ours went out on his balcony. I asked them to call management in order to open my door.

They came but could not open it. Finally after the fourth hour, the locksmith arrived, and I was set free! Now when I go anywhere with a balcony, I put a wedge in the balcony doors! Lol

Patty C

"The Lord now said to Moses, "Send out men to explore the land of Canaan, the land I am giving to the Israelites. Send one leader from each of the twelve ancestral tribes." So Moses did as the Lord commanded him. He sent out twelve men, all tribal leaders of Israel, from their camp in the wilderness of Paran."

"After exploring the land for forty days, the men returned...This was their report to Moses: "We entered the land you sent us to explore, and it is indeed a bountiful country—a land flowing with milk and honey. Here is the kind of fruit it produces. But the people living there are powerful, and their towns are large and fortified. We even saw giants there, the descendants of Anak!

But Caleb tried to quiet the people as they stood before Moses. "Let's go at once to take the land," he said. "We can certainly conquer it!" But the other men who had explored the land with him disagreed. "We can't go up against them! They are stronger than we are!" So they spread this bad report about the land among the Israelites: "The land we traveled through and explored will devour anyone who goes to live there. All the people we saw were huge."

"Then the whole community began weeping aloud, and they cried all night. Their voices rose in a great chorus of protest against Moses and Aaron. "If only we had died in Egypt, or even here in the wilderness!" they complained.

Then Moses and Aaron fell face down on the ground before the whole community of Israel. Two of the men who had explored the land, Joshua son of Nun and Caleb son of Jephunneh, tore their *clothing. They said to all the people of Israel, "The land we traveled through and explored is a wonderful land! And if the Lord is pleased with us, he will bring us safely into that land and give it to us. It is a rich land flowing with milk and honey. Do not rebel against the Lord, and don't be afraid of the people of the land. They are only helpless prey to us! They have no protection, but the Lord is with us! Don't be afraid of them!" But the whole community began to talk about stoning Joshua and Caleb. Then the glorious presence of the Lord appeared to all the Israelites at the Tabernacle." (Numbers 13:1-3, 25, 27-28, 30-32; 14:1-2, 5-10)*

Twelve spies were sent to explore the land God was about to deliver into their hands as their inheritance. All twelve saw the same things, but only two looked through "different lenses."

When Joshua and Caleb tried to encourage the people to put their faith in God, they were met with resistance and death threats. It's hard to believe after all the people had witnessed in their deliverance from Egypt, they still would not allow themselves to surrender and trust God's leading and promises!

Once again, Moses and Aaron find themselves face down on the ground interceding between a rebellious, unfaithful people and an angry God. It was because of this very disbelief that judgment would come to the entire nation to wander in the wilderness for forty years until all who were twenty years and older died.

Their fear strangled even the hopes of the innocent who did believe, Joshua and Caleb, for another forty years. How frustrating it must have been for them after seeing the goodness and bounty of the land God promised and after trusting and surrendering to God's leading, that they too be included in the judgment of the unfaithful.

Have you ever found yourself in a situation due to the behavior or beliefs of others, you too became part of a judgment and were not able to fulfill or live out a promise? What did you do? How did you react?

The stronghold of fear knows no boundaries, nor is it a respecter of persons. Fear is never a planned nor invited guest but comes unexpectedly. Like any intruder it can leave us hopeless, weak, and vulnerable. Fear, itself, may come unexpectedly but we still have a choice to make it comfortable...to surrender our heart's home to it.

Fear changes the landscape of our hearts. Where once we produced rich fruit, we became frozen. Trust was replaced with worry, and hope was replaced with despair. But just as in winter when fruit trees hibernate until spring's warmth and rain, fear need not be a death threat for our tomorrow. When fear comes knocking at our door, let the Spirit of God answer with Truth.

In the military, when an enlisted man/woman captures an enemy, he does not try to reason with him but rather secures the enemy as a captive and does not release him until he is placed into the hands of a superior.

This is the thought behind 2 Corinthians 10:3-5:

> *"For though we live in the world, we do not wage war as the world does. The weapons we fight with are not the weapons of the world. On the contrary, they have divine power to demolish strongholds. We demolish arguments and every pretension that sets itself up against the knowledge of God, and we take captive every thought to make it obedient to Christ."* (*NIV*)

Fear starts in our thoughts, in our mind. We have the choice to entertain them or take them captive. As soon as those thoughts come, we subject them to the Truth of God's Word. If they fail to align to what God says as truth, then we literally treat them like an enemy and release them to our Superior, God. There are times when I need to do this verbally and other times when I silently release those thoughts that are lies. The catch is, we must know the Truth before we can distinguish it from a lie.

Jesus gave us a wonderful example to follow in His reaction to Satan's temptation in the wilderness. Jesus didn't reason with him. Rather, with each testing and each falsehood, He replied, "It is written." On the night of Jesus' arrest in the garden, His mind must have been overloaded with demonic activity bombarding His resolve to finish what God sent Him to do.

Fear thrives on opportunity to intensify its stronghold. Fear was at the root of all the emotions Adam and Eve experienced when their eyes and senses were opened to the devastating results of their disobedience.

FAITH IS A WEAPON IN OUR ARSENAL AGAINST FEAR

The Lord sent Isaiah to deliver a message to Judah's King Ahaz in Isaiah chapters 7-8. We learn the following about Ahaz from 2 Kings 16 and 2 Chronicles 28:

1. His father Jotham was a powerful king of Judah because he was careful to live in obedience to the Lord his God.

2. Ahaz was 20 years old when he became king of Judah (King Pekah was in his 17th year of reign in Israel) and reigned 16 years.

3. "Hezekiah, his son, ruled after him and did what was pleasing in the Lord's sight. There was no one like him among all the kings of Judah, either before or after his time. He remained faithful to the Lord in everything and he was careful to obey all the commands the Lord had given Moses." (2 Kings 18)

4. Ahaz was not a good, righteous king; he even sacrificed his own son through fire. He followed detestable pagan practices and sacrifices. He would even close the doors to the Lord's temple so no one could worship there. He set up pagan altars in every corner of Jerusalem.

5. Because Ahaz encouraged his people to sin, God allowed the kings of Aram and Israel to attack him. Instead of humbling himself before God, Ahaz made a pact with the king of Syria to rescue him from these two armies, thereby going into servitude (even giving valuable articles of the Temple as tribute) to Assyria. It backfired because the king of Syria attacked Ahaz instead of helping him.

6. When Ahaz died, he was buried in Jerusalem but not in the royal cemetery of the kings of Judah.

ISAIAH 7:1-9

"When Ahaz, son of Jotham and grandson of Uzziah, was king of Judah, King Rezin of Syria and Pekah son of Remaliah, the king of Israel, set out to attack Jerusalem. However, they were unable to carry out their plan. The news had come to the royal court of Judah: 'Syria is allied with Israel against us!' So the hearts of the king and his people trembled with fear, like trees shaking in a storm. Then the Lord said to Isaiah, 'Take your son Shear-jashub and go out to meet King Ahaz. You will find him at the end of the aqueduct that feeds water into the upper pool, near the road leading to the field where cloth is washed. Tell him to stop worrying. Tell him he doesn't need to fear the fierce anger of those two burned-out embers, King Rezin of Syria and Pekah son of Remaliah. Yes, the kings of Syria and Israel are plotting against him, saying, "We will attack Judah and capture it for ourselves. Then we will install the son of Tabeel as Judah's king." But this is what the Sovereign Lord says: "This invasion will never happen; it will never take place; for Syria is no stronger than its capital, Damascus, and Damascus is no stronger than its king, Rezin. As for Israel, within sixty-five years it will be crushed and completely destroyed. Israel is no stronger than its capital, Samaria, and Samaria is no stronger than its king, Pekah son of Remaliah. Unless your faith is firm, I cannot make you stand firm'"."

HOW THIS RELATES TO US TODAY

1. We can all relate to bad news. No one is immune from it. We get a bad report from the doctor, court hearing, work review, etc. that is not what we were expecting or anticipating. It catches us off guard.

2. Like King Ahaz, *"...the hearts of the king and his people trembled with fear.",* fear can either motivate us to action or paralyze us; it can blind us to truth and instead we dwell on the negative. Our fear can infect others around us with fear. The people were looking to their king for direction, and he was literally trembling in his boots!!

3. The Lord *knew exactly where Ahaz was* and sent His messenger to him.

   - Aqueducts were not only a source of water for a city but also could be the place of compromise, thereby allowing the enemy access to a walled and gated city.
   - Ahaz was not only shaking in fear from the impending attack but wanted to make sure he wasn't giving an enemy open access to the city via its source of water.
   - Perhaps he recognized that through his neglect, this was the place that needed fortifying due to disrepair or decay. That would have only increased his level of fear. Ahaz just didn't have time!
   - Can you not see him pacing like a caged animal trying to bark out orders while trying to maintain his composure in front of his people and failing miserably at both!

4. I LOVE that *God met him at his place of fear*!
   When we get a bad report are we so trembling with fear that we don't...or can't see...or hear God meeting us *in* the

place of our fear? Our fear, our trembling does NOT scare God away!

5. VS 4-5 *"Tell him to stop worrying."* When fear encompasses our thoughts and actions, we can't think straight and see clearly. God's encouragement is *always* on time. But we can miss it due to fear, worry, and trying to plan our attack.

Philippians 4:6-9 "Don't worry about anything; instead, pray about everything. Tell God what you need, and thank him for all he has done. Then you will experience God's peace, which exceeds anything we can understand. His peace will guard your hearts and minds as you live in Christ Jesus. And now, dear brothers and sisters, one final thing. Fix your thoughts on what is true, and honorable, and right, and pure, and lovely, and admirable. Think about things that are excellent and worthy of praise. Keep putting into practice all you learned and received from me—everything you heard from me and saw me doing. Then the God of peace will be with you."
(Philippians 4:6-9)

- Peace is the opposite of fear.
- Hope is the opposite of despair.
- Prayer is the opposite of worry.
- Conflict becomes the fertile soil for peace, hope, and prayer to grow.

David gives us a beautiful contrast from Ahaz in responding to a bad report in these excerpts from

Psalm 27: *"The Lord is my light and my salvation— so why should I be afraid? The Lord is my fortress, protecting me from danger, so why should I tremble? When evil people come to devour me, when my enemies and foes attack me, they will stumble and fall. Though a mighty army surrounds me, my heart will not be afraid. Even if I am attacked, I will remain confident.*

Then I will hold my head high above my enemies who surround me. At his sanctuary I will offer sacrifices with shouts of joy, singing and praising the Lord with music.

Yet I am confident I will see the Lord's goodness while I am here in the land of the living. Wait patiently for the Lord. Be brave and courageous. Yes, wait patiently for the Lord." (Psalm 27:1-3, 6, 13-14)

6. *"Tell him he doesn't need to fear the fierce anger of those two* <u>*burned-out embers (THEY HAVE NO POWER)*</u>*…..Yes they are plotting against him, saying…BUT THIS IS WHAT THE SOVEREIGN LORD SAYS"*

VS. 7b *"This invasion will never happen; it will never take place...in fact, Israel will be crushed and completely destroyed within 65 years from now."*

We again look to David for a beautiful contrast:

"The Lord frustrates the plans of the nations and thwarts all their schemes. But the Lord's plans stand firm forever; his intentions can never be shaken. The Lord looks down from heaven and sees the whole human race. From his throne he observes all who live on the earth. He made their hearts, so he understands everything they do. The

best-equipped army cannot save a king, nor is great strength enough to save a warrior. Don't count on your warhorse to give you victory— for all its strength, it cannot save you. But the Lord watches over those who fear him, those who rely on his unfailing love. He rescues them from death and keeps them alive in times of famine. We put our hope in the Lord. He is our help and our shield. In him our hearts rejoice, for we trust in his holy name. Let your unfailing love surround us, Lord, for our hope is in you alone." (Psalm 33:10-11, 13-22)

STANDING FIRM IN FAITH CANNOT BE FORCED

--*"Unless your faith is firm, I CANNOT MAKE YOU STAND FIRM."* Isaiah 7:9b NLT

--*"If you will not believe, Surely you shall not be established."* Isaiah 7:9 NKJV

--*"If you will not believe [and trust in God and His message], be assured that you will not be established."* Isaiah 7:9 AMP

The Hebrew word for "established" means to support, confirm, be faithful, uphold, be carried (I.e., "pillars are supporters of the door").

Standing faith will never be something that is taught or handed down but must be experienced. This will only happen as we go through trials, hardships, and even times of seemingly silence from God.

- God cannot force us to have standing faith.
- Faith, standing faith, is a choice.
- Firm faith is a process.

- Faith is foundational to our minds being quiet, resting, and standing firm even in the midst of uncertainty and in the midst of bad reports.

Hebrews 11:1 "Faith is the confidence that what we hope for will actually happen; it gives us assurance about things we cannot see."

Even though Ahaz *"did not follow in the ways of the Lord,"* God was still willing, longing...still wanted to **"support and carry"** *(as in the Hebrew meaning above)* Ahaz.

2 Chronicles 28:22,25,27 *"Even during this time of trouble, King Ahaz continued to reject the Lord...he aroused the anger of the Lord, the God of his ancestors...When he died he was not buried in the royal cemetery of the kings of Judah."* What a sad reflection of his life.

WE ARE IMAGE BEARERS OF THE ONE IN WHOM WE PLACE OUR FAITH

Jesus said, *"No one can serve two masters. For you will hate one and love the other; you will be devoted to one and despise the other. You cannot serve God and be enslaved to money...That is why I tell you not to worry about everyday life— whether you have enough food and drink, or enough clothes to wear. Isn't life more than food, and your body more than clothing? These things dominate the thoughts of unbelievers, but your heavenly Father already knows all your needs. Seek the Kingdom of God above all else, and live righteously, and he will give you everything you need."* (Matthew 6:24-25, 32-33)

In chapter three of my "Tchotchke"[13] Bible Study, we discovered what being in "the image" of someone meant. When God created us in His own image (Genesis 1:26-27), the word "image" in the Hebrew is *elc* and comes from an unused root meaning "to shade; likeness (of resemblance)."

> "Keep me as the apple of your eye; Hide me in the *shadow* (Hebrew 'lc , the same root as 'elc' in "image") of your wings." (Psalm 17:8)

> Think of summer when the sun is out and creates a shadow (a "resemblance") of an object. We are never in front of that shadow but always under. To be shaded by something or someone means to be protected much like an umbrella protects us while we are walking through a storm.

> When the Israelites worshipped other gods, those other gods never "protected/shaded" their worshipers. Those gods were, and still are, powerless to protect!

> From the very beginning man was never meant or created to take the place of God...
> - Never meant to *lead* in front of God
> - Never meant to be the one *providing* the shade

---

[13] Tchotchke: What we tend to hold onto in our lives that prevent us from really living! Chapter three, pg 30
https://www.amazon.com/dp/172784257X/ref=cm_sw_r_cp_tai_Bh6aDb6MX051R

- Never meant to be *equal* to God
- We were *always* meant to be "led by God"
- We were *always* meant to be "under God's sovereign control"

...because "in the shadow, the resemblance of God" is where we find our protection, peace and identity! (Psalm 121)

Our actions, speech, and the very countenance of our appearance will reveal the image of whom we put our faith in when times of difficulties and uncertainties come our way.

We cannot, as Jesus said, serve faith and fear at the same time.

In Isaiah 8:11-20, God told Isaiah not to get caught up in Ahaz and Israel's fear. They are great words for us to follow today:

- Don't think like everyone else.
- Don't live in dread and fear of what frightens others.
- Make the Lord of Heaven's armies holy in your life.
- Fear God. He is the One Who should make you tremble. He will make you safe.
- Preserve the teaching of God; entrust His instructions to those who follow Him.
- Wait for the Lord; put your hope in Him.
- Look to God for guidance, instruction, and teachings.

Where are you with fear, worry, and anxiety? To whom, in whom, or in what are you placing your confidence? Is it a "sure foundation?"

Unless our faith is firm in Jesus Christ, as with Ahaz God cannot make our faith firm and impenetrable. He cannot make us believe. He cannot support and carry us if we do not allow Him to do so.

I pray you make God, not fear, your refuge and stronghold.

HOMEWORK = link between what we have <u>learned</u> and what we <u>think</u> about, which results in what we put into <u>practice</u>

Memorize these verses as part of your "weapons that have divine power to demolish strongholds" in your life:
2Timothy 1:7
2 Corinthians 10:3-5

According to Psalm 34:4-8, 17-19 what happens when we give our fear through prayer to the Lord?

Chapter Nine
A Pleasing Aroma...Leviticus 23

Your unfailing love is better than life itself; how I praise you!
I will praise you as long as I live, lifting up
my hands to you in prayer.
You satisfy me more than the richest feast.
I will praise you with songs of joy.
Psalm 63:3-5

Aren't we there yet??

Amazing how often when in traffic people cut us off or make sudden changes without signaling ahead of time - and how quickly it catches us off guard. Sometimes these sudden changes cause accidents, and sometimes if we are alert enough we avoid a disaster. I often get angry - kind of taking the offense personally; which is so silly because I don't even know that person. God has softened me with "Love always hopes" (I Corinthians 13), and I try to think that maybe they're in a hurry for an important reason or maybe they're distraught about something and are distracted because of it.
Lori M

I love gathering with friends around a table of food! Rich conversations, laughter, encouragement, reminiscing about memories, and oh the food! It can be a smorgasbord of wonderful delicacies, home style comfort food, dessert and coffee, or simple finger foods. Food always seems to taste better when it's shared with friends, not to mention we usually eat more when talking with friends! Add church banquets, work-related dinners, and holidays spent with family and friends, and we can definitely say a significant part of what we do focuses around eating.

The aroma of the feast is just as important as the feasting itself. Before my husband and I downsized our house, we would have my entire family (usually around 30 people) over for Thanksgiving Day dinner. I would put the turkey in the oven the night before on slow roast. Oh the aroma of that bird throughout the night!! The meat would fall off the bone and was so juicy...my mouth is salivating as I write this!

Feasts played a large role for the Israelites in how they worshipped and honored God. There are five special feasts listed in Exodus and Deuteronomy:

1. Passover and the Feast of Unleavened Bread (Exodus 34; Deuteronomy 16; Numbers 9 and 28; Leviticus 23)
2. Feast of Weeks also known as Harvest of Firstfruits (Deuteronomy 16; Leviticus 23; Numbers 28), this was also the Day of Pentecost in Acts.
3. Feasts of Trumpets (Leviticus 23; Numbers 29), modernly called Rosh Hashanah.
4. Day of Atonement (Leviticus 16 and 23; Numbers 29), celebrated today as Yom Kippur.
5. Feast of Tabernacles...Booths or Ingathering (Leviticus 23; Numbers 29; Deuteronomy 16)

How do these feasts relate to us today?

I am not suggesting we raid somebody's farm and start sacrificing animals or their grain, but I believe we can learn from what the Lord required of the Israelites in remembering and honoring him.

They were to set aside these days as special events, days of rest, and in the process offering a pleasing aroma to the Lord.

Did Jesus not tell us to come to Him and lay our burdens on Him and He would give us rest?

Rest requires waiting, and waiting is hard. I don't particularly like waiting! It's not that I shy away from the process of a challenge or new ideas, but I also like action and resolution. Waiting is especially hard when it is in silence. Am I supposed to be doing something or perhaps nothing, and if so what direction should I or shouldn't I take? If I'm not careful my mind will go into overtime seeking direction when the only direction I am to be taking is...waiting.

The act of waiting can be the difference between microwave cooking and crock-pot cooking. There are advantages to both, but depending on the end result sometimes one is better than the other.

- Microwave cooking is quick and always has the background sound of the microwave working so you know something is happening.

- Crock-pot cooking is silent and would seem as though nothing is happening until the wonderful aroma of whatever is slow cooking starts to permeate the room.

I usually make roast beef in my crock pot with plenty of onions, garlic, and other seasonings and veggies. Raw onions and garlic are too potent and bitter for my taste, but when mixed with the roast and slow cooked all day their flavors soften and enhance an amazing taste to the beef.

Life's heartaches and trials are like onions and garlic; left raw they are offensive, burn, and bring tears at times. If they are not dealt with, we can give off a horrible smell to those around us. When we allow the Holy Spirit to work through them in our hearts, we learn amazing lessons and compassion. They add flavor and aromas that draw others to His grace and mercy. This takes time...waiting.

It is in the waiting our hardened hearts receive the tenderizing of 'Holy Spirit slow cooking' in order for the extravagant grace and mercy of God to be seen (smelled) in the world around us. In waiting comes the promise, "*You will keep in perfect peace all who trust in you, all whose thoughts are fixed on you!*" (Isaiah 26:3) May we not be in such a hurry for quick fixes that we miss the sweet aroma Christ is trying to produce in us through our waiting times.

They were to deny themselves.

In the description of these feasts I specifically noticed the statement "deny yourselves." Isn't this the main focus in our worship of God, to deny ourselves? To surrender ourselves as a living sacrifice to God? To be that sweet aroma offering to God and to others around us of Who God is? That is the very essence of living, and yet it is the very essence of death resulting in denying our wants, our ways, and the satisfaction of our cravings.

> "Do not love this world nor the things it offers you, for when you love the world, you do not have the love of the Father in you. For the world offers only a craving for physical pleasure, a craving for everything we see, and pride in our achievements and possessions. These are not from the Father, but are from this world. And this world is fading away, along with everything that people crave. But anyone who does what pleases God will live forever." (1 John 2:15-17)

The problem with cravings is they are never satisfied. May we say as David did,

> "Satisfy us each morning with your unfailing love, so we may sing for joy to the end of our lives." (Psalms 90:14)

They were to give proportionate to God's blessings.

No one was to come empty-handed, and the gifts were to be in proportion to the way the Lord blessed them. There wasn't any "flat rate" percentage, always calculating to make sure we are obedient to the penny without going overboard! I wonder what would happen in our lives today, how God would respond and provide, if we gave recklessly to God. What if we would be bold enough to give a blank check, trusting God to set the limit within the "priest (treasurer)" who would receive it. What about giving to those in need when we are about our daily activities? Do you carry an extra $5, $10, $20, or perhaps a $50 in your wallet, not in case you find a good deal for you, but ready when you sense God's directing to give to a complete stranger?

What if God blessed us in proportion to what we give back to Him? Paul carried this theme when he wrote the Corinthians:

"Now I want you to know, dear brothers and sisters, what God in his kindness has done through the churches in Macedonia. They are being tested by many troubles, and they are very poor. But they are also filled with abundant joy, which has overflowed in rich generosity....

Since you excel in so many ways—in your faith, your gifted speakers, your knowledge, your enthusiasm, and your love from us —I want you to excel also in this gracious act of giving...You know the generous grace of our Lord Jesus Christ. Though he was rich, yet for your sakes he became poor, so that by his poverty he could make you rich...Let the eagerness you showed in the beginning be matched now by your giving. Give in proportion to what you have. Whatever you give is acceptable if you give it eagerly. And give according to what you have, not what you don't have. Of course, I don't mean your giving should make life easy for others and hard for yourselves...Right now you have plenty and can help those who are in need. Later, they will have plenty and can share with you when you need it. In this way, things will be equal." (2 Corinthians 8:1-2, 7, 9, 11-14)

They were to have purposeful feasting and sacrifice.

Webster defines sacrifice as, "a giving up, destroying, etc. of one thing for the sake of another of higher value."[14] The priest didn't just go haphazardly into the presence of God to offer the sacrifice. There was a process, a purpose, thought involved of what they were going to do. There was a reverence for Whom they were approaching. I sometimes think we forget about that in our modern day idea of what it means to worship God, to enter into His presence. _We_ don't do God a favor by showing up. _He_ looks upon us with favor in His presence. He looks into our hearts to view our motive in entering His presence.

Do we prepare the night before, perhaps God awakens us during the night, do we anticipate entering and "feasting" on the Lord? Do we ready our hearts to hear from Him prior to even touching the door of His sanctuary? I know we are all in different seasons of our lives. Wherever life finds us, we all need to find time proportionate to the demands on our lives, to be purposeful in our worship.

Holy incense

"Place the incense altar just outside the inner curtain that shields the Ark of the Covenant, in front of the Ark's cover—the place of atonement—that covers the tablets

---

[14] Concise Edition, Webster's New World Dictionary of the American Language © 1956, The World Publishing Company

*inscribed with the terms of the covenant. **I will meet with you there. Every morning** when Aaron maintains the lamps, he must burn fragrant incense on the altar. **And each evening when he lights the lamps, he must again burn incense in the Lord's presence.** This must be done from generation to generation. Do not offer any unholy incense on this altar, or any burnt offerings, grain offerings, or liquid offerings. **Once a year Aaron must purify the altar by smearing its horns with blood from the offering made to purify the people from their sin. This will be a regular, annual event from generation to generation, for this is the Lord's most holy altar."* (Exodus 30:6-10 bold added)

Jesus fulfilled the requirements and purpose of the incense in His life and death. Hebrews chapter 5 describes how the High Priest represents the people in their dealings with God and he must be called by God for His work.

*"**Every high priest is a man chosen to represent other people in their dealings with God**. He presents their gifts to God and **offers sacrifices for their sins**...And no one can become a high priest simply because he wants such an honor. **He must be called by God for this work, just as Aaron was.** That is why **Christ did not honor himself by assuming he could become High Priest. No, he was chosen by God,** who said to him.."* (Hebrews 5:1, 4-5 bold added)

*"**While Jesus was here on earth, he offered prayers and pleadings, with a loud cry and tears,** to the one*

*who could rescue him from death. And God heard his prayers because of his deep reverence for God. Even though Jesus was God's Son, he learned obedience from the things he suffered. In this way, **God qualified him as a perfect High Priest, and he became the source of eternal salvation for all those who obey him.** And God designated him to be a High Priest in the order of Melchizedek." (Hebrews 5:7-10 bold added)*

Jesus knew exactly what His purpose and mission in coming to earth was:

- He came to destroy the works of the devil. (1 John 3:8b)
- Christ became our High Priest, the only One Who could enter the Holy of Holies. (Hebrews 7:16; 9:11)
- With His own blood, he entered the Most Holy of Holies once for all time securing our redemption forever. (Hebrews 9:12, 28; 10:5-18)
- His purified the "heavenly Tabernacle" with his blood. (Hebrews 9:23-26)
- His prayers on earth, night and morning, were the holy incense burned before God. (Hebrews 5:7; John 17)
- Because Jesus fulfilled these requirements, we now have direct access into the Holy of Holies, into the very presence of God (Hebrews 10:19-22)
- In fact, God's very presence, His Holy Spirit lives inside any who have called on the name of the Lord for salvation. (John 14:15-21)

Incense is used interchangeably with devotion and prayer. David said:

> "Accept my prayer as incense offered to you, and my upraised hands as an evening offering." (Psalms 141:2)

The formula for incense was special and not to be used personally, only in worshiping God. (Exodus 30:34-38; Leviticus 10:1-3) Unfortunately, Israel repeatedly prostituted themselves before other gods and used what was holy in their worship of other gods.

> "'For Israel has forsaken me and turned this valley into a place of wickedness. The people burn incense to foreign gods—idols never before acknowledged by this generation, by their ancestors, or by the kings of Judah. And they have filled this place with the blood of innocent children." (Jeremiah 19:4)

Revelation 5:8 refers to, "gold bowls filled with incense, which are the prayers of God's people." What does our incense look like today? Do we struggle with our prayer life? Are we of one mind when we meet corporately for worship and prayer? Are we focused or does our mind wander? How about in our quiet times, when no one is "leading us" in prayer, when it's just us and God? Hebrews 7:24-25 tells us:

> "But because Jesus lives forever, his priesthood lasts forever. Therefore he is able, once and forever, to save those who come to God through him. He lives forever to intercede with God on their behalf."

Are we actively participating in Jesus' intercession for us? In bringing our prayers, waiting expectantly for His direction and answers?

Will our prayers be a sweet and pleasing aroma to God? Or will they be like the unholy incense Israel offered to pagan gods? Do we struggle to stay true to God rather than worship idols of "want, personal gain, money, or approval by society?" Do we worship and reverently fear God for Who He is and what He has done for us or view him as the genie in the sky?

I don't ask these questions to bring guilt and condemnation. We all have fallen into one or more of these questionable prayer dimensions. Rather I'm trying to encourage and stimulate us into God righteousness. This is not impossible!

I pray that when we've fallen prostrate before our God in Heaven, we won't sense a loss for not taking prayer more seriously...the spiritual battle fought on earth more seriously...the awesome privilege of confiding, trusting, expecting, and offering sweet incense to God more seriously than we did.

Holy. Set apart. Waiting. Incense, sweet aroma rising up to God's nostrils, acceptable and pleasing to Him.

Author and speaker Nancy Leigh DeMoss describes the story of a mother's sweet aroma in her son's life in her book, "A Place of Quiet Rest"[15]. His mother habitually began each day,

---

[15] A Place of Quiet Rest, Finding Intimacy With God Through A Daily

before her household awakened, in reading the Bible, prayer, and meditation. It was through this practice that she gained her strength, sweetness and grace to face the challenges of the day.

I don't know about you, but oh how I want my family, friends, and neighbors to remember me by the aroma of grace, mercy, kindness, gentleness, goodness, love, joy, patience, peace, and self control. I want the sweet fruit from time spent in His presence to permeate a world looking for these in all the wrong places.

HOMEWORK = link between what we have <u>learned</u> and what we <u>think</u> about, which results in what we put into <u>practice</u>

1. Write a song of praise to God. It doesn't have to be pages and pages, although it might end up to be. Start with one sentence. The end goal is that it comes from YOUR heart...it's YOUR sweet praise to God.
2. What has God revealed to you about His heart, character? Has he delivered you from something? Has he healed you from something?
    -OR-
    Is He in the process of doing these, or something else and you need to thank Him IN ADVANCE Philippians 4:6-8; Colossians 1:9-29; Ephesians 1:3-14

Devotional Life, © 2000, Moody Press, Chicago, IL, page 256

3. Sing your favorite scripture verse. This is just to be between you and God! So make a joyful "noise" unto the Lord! As with a loving parent, being on key, musically-theory correct doesn't matter...it's the sweet aroma from your heart that will bring a smile to God's face!

4. Read the Psalms

"Remember that worship, praise, and thanksgiving are a response to God's revelation of himself. As he shows himself to you and speaks to you through his Word, you will find yourself wanting to respond to him in praise for who he is and what he has done." [16]

---

[16] Ibid, page 219

Chapter Ten
Coming Into a Good Land...Deuteronomy 8:7, 11:8-15

What joy for those whose strength comes from the Lord,
who have set their minds on a pilgrimage to Jerusalem.
When they walk through the Valley of Weeping,
it will become a place of refreshing springs.
The autumn rains will clothe it with blessings.
They will continue to grow stronger,
and each of them will appear before God in Jerusalem.
Psalm 84:5-7

Aren't we there yet??

My sisters and I were very excited about heading to Florida with our family for the week of Thanksgiving break. We were in the truck pulling a camper behind us when my sister said, "I won't believe it till I get there." As we passed Gettysburg, PA, having been on the road for a short time, the alternator light came on in the truck. My dad didn't do anything about it until we reached the Carolina's. We needed a new alternator, so we stopped at a motel for the night while they fixed it. Since it was Thanksgiving we had our planned Thanksgiving meal in the motel. The next morning, after a new alternator was installed, off we went. Or so we thought! We only went several miles when the light came back on. My dad decided to turn around and go back to the garage so the mechanic could check into it again. After much discussion the old alternator was put back into the truck, and we headed home. We were not happy to say the least and never made it to Florida! As we were almost home and passing Gettysburg again, the light turned off. I guess we were not meant to go to Florida. We did, however, make the trip several years later. To this day we talk about the time we almost went to Florida and how my sister's comment actually came true.

Tina B

"But you will cross the Jordan and settle in the land the Lord your God is giving you as an inheritance, and he will give you rest from all your enemies around you so that you will live in safety." *(Deuteronomy 12:10)*

"Don't let your hearts be troubled. Trust in God, and trust also in me. There is more than enough room in my Father's home. If this were not so, would I have told you that I am going to prepare a place for you? When everything is ready, I will come and get you, so that you will always be with me where I am...And you know the way to where I am going... I am the Way, the Truth, and the Life. No one can come to the Father except through me." *(John 14:1-6)*

Have you ever planned...and planned...and planned some more for the most amazing vacation you could ever dream of taking? Did you Google all the reviews and perhaps talk to a travel agent to get all the brochures so you wouldn't miss any adventure while there?

I remember one particular vacation we had at a resort in Jamaica years ago. We were told by the travel agent it would be the most incredible place we could visit...as long as we stayed within the perimeters of the resort.

No matter where we venture out to, there are going to be boundaries for our own safety. We wouldn't think of walking alone, at night, down the streets of any big town. Boundaries are good and necessary for safety and freedom. We tend to think boundaries are inhibitors to freedom when in reality they assure safety in freedom.

Life has boundaries. Our bodies have boundaries. We were never meant to live forever in these bodies or on this Earth. Aging has been something we work hard at to never accomplish. Hollywood, cosmetic companies, and health gurus persuade us we can live longer...live better...reclaim our youth...be happy if we just buy into their products and lifestyles. Ironic how much of our speech, time, and money is spent to avoid the God-instilled boundaries of life and to reverse the very avenue by which we will fulfill this journey called life. Death is as much a part of life as life is a part of death.

Even Earth has boundaries and limits to its existence (Job 38:4-11; Psalm 24:1-2). While we are to take care of this temporary home God has given us (Genesis 1:28, 2:15; Psalm 24:1), there will be an end to this earth (2 Peter 3:10; Matthew 24:29,35; Revelation 21:1).

VACATIONS ARE TEMPORARY...EARTH IS A TEMPORARY RESIDENCE

Throughout Scripture we are reminded that earth is not our permanent home (Hebrews 13:14). References like "we are aliens living it in a foreign land" bear witness to this fact (1 Peter 1:17, 2:11). A vacation is only a temporary visit. It is not permanent. Perhaps it would be more fitting to look at our life on earth as a temporary work assignment, which would be more in line with "aliens in a foreign land."

If attitudes reveal the heart, is vacation, self-indulgence and pleasure seeking more our purpose or goal in life than fulfilling our God-given destiny? I'm not against having fun and enjoying the good God has provided or partaking in much-needed rest. The beauty and majesty of pounding waves upon the beach or the lavish colors and artistic sprays of sunset over the ocean; the rolling hills, mountains, and awakening of spring with freshness in the air and the promise of life; and the glorious array of autumn colors in themselves declare the glory and splendor of our Creator! These are to be enjoyed!

> *"God has made everything beautiful for its own time. He has planted eternity in the human heart, but even so, people cannot see the whole scope of God's work from beginning to end."* (Ecclesiastes 3:11)

But do we live as though this is all that we have...that this *is* life?

God put a longing in our hearts for something more than what we have here and now. Could it be that this longing for something new, a different scenery, a respite from the daily grind of work, of just existing is all part of "eternity He has planted in our hearts?" That somewhere in the depths of our hearts we know this world is not and cannot fill the longing of the presence, peace, and safety of God? Cannot fill the longing of being cared for like a child comforted by a daddy safe in the snuggle of his lap with his arms wrapped around them? Cannot fill the longing for permanence and total satisfaction?

So close...Deuteronomy 34:1-4

The journey has been long. The God Who promised, led, and fulfilled His promises for a land flowing with milk and honey has been faithful. Moses is now at the end of his personal journey.

Let's take a few moments and ponder what Moses may have been processing:

- Moses had been intimately involved with God in the most minute details of this journey to the Promised Land.
- Details about the worship of God, constructing, setting up, and tearing down of the Tabernacle...the very place God would dwell and speak to Moses and in the future to the priests.
- Details regarding their relationship with God, with each other, and with foreigners with whom they would come in contact.
- Details regarding that which is clean and unclean, both dietary and physical.

- Privileges and consequences of disobedience when they get to the Promised Land.
- His personal journey in faith and trust...and his personal failures.
- Perhaps regret for his own disobedience that cost him entry into the very destination in which he had been so deeply invested and involved and for which he longed.

Can you imagine everything that was involved in this journey...and then stopping short of the delight and excitement of experiencing of stepping foot into this Promised Land?!

It would be like planning the most amazing journey along with the anticipation of the experience only to be told at the gate to the plane, "sorry your ticket is invalid...no entry...at ANY time!"

Moses escorted the people to the very edge and then had to say "goodbye." (Yes, he is going to a "better" Promised Land, but this is the one he had been anticipating.) It was his last day on Earth, and Moses climbed Mount Nebo to get a long-awaited view of the Promised Land. Behind him are the people that he has led, loved, been frustrated with, and pled with God for His mercy. He knows first hand God can deliver them from their enemies when they cross over and also knows they will struggle with maintaining their covenant relationship with Him. He knows the consequences they will have to bear because of their impending disobedience.

I can only speculate his heart is full of thanksgiving, full of unexplainable joy, full of memories, and full of regret and sorrow when he ascends Mount Nebo, never to return. His feet measuring every step, his ears hearing every beat of his heart, his eyes surveying every inch of his path trying to stamp into his memory. Going forward yet hesitating as he soaks in every second.

Moses knew his last day. We don't. If we did, what would your final thoughts be? My final thoughts?

> *"When Moses had finished giving these instructions to all the people of Israel, he said, "I am now 120 years old, and I am no longer able to lead you. The Lord has told me, 'You will not cross the Jordan River.' But the Lord your God himself will cross over ahead of you. He will destroy the nations living there, and you will take possession of their land. Joshua will lead you across the river, just as the Lord promised." (Deuteronomy 31:1-3)*
>
> *"So Moses, the servant of the Lord, died there in Moab, as the Lord had said. The Lord buried him in Moab… Moses was 120 years old when he died, yet his eyesight was clear and he was as strong as ever."*
>
> *(Deuteronomy 34:5-7)*

Earth is not our final chapter, our resting place…

In many ways we are to be like Moses to our world today. We, like Moses, are to be the voice of Truth in a world filled with the false worship of self-serving gods and idols; always leading and pointing others to the One True and Living God; always interceding on their behalf; relationally involved on the path to our Promised Land.

"We must quickly carry out the tasks assigned us by the one who sent us. The night is coming, and then no one can work." (John 9:4)

Jesus' command and promise for us to be a Moses:

"Go into all the world and preach the good news to everyone. Anyone who believes and is baptized will be saved. But anyone who refuses to believe will be condemned. These miraculous signs will accompany those who believe: They will cast out demons in my name, and they will speak in new languages. They will be able to handle snakes with safety, and if they drink anything poisonous, it won't hurt them. They will be able to place their hands on the sick, and they will be healed...And the disciples went everywhere and preached, and the Lord worked through them, confirming what they said by many miraculous signs." (Mark 16:15-18, 20)

And just as Moses declared to God, "I will not go if your presence doesn't go before me," we too must wait on God's Holy Spirit to lead and guide us in our journey (Acts 1:4-5, 8).

John said in 1 John 3:2-3; 1 John 5:21

"Dear friends, we are already God's children, but he has not yet shown us what we will be like when Christ appears. But we do know that we will be like him, for we will see him as he really is. And all who have this eager expectation will keep themselves pure, just as he is pure...Dear children, keep away from anything that might take God's place in your hearts."

God has so much more for us. Why do we settle for less?

We are here to invest...

Deuteronomy 34:9 (NIV), *"Now Joshua son of Nun was filled with the spirit of wisdom because Moses had laid his hands on him. So the Israelites listened to him and did what the Lord had commanded Moses."*

Whom are we leading, raising up, and investing in so "you may lay your hands upon" as your predecessors in the faith?

Moses invested in Joshua

Elijah invested in Elisha

Paul invested in Timothy

Naomi invested in Ruth

YOU are investing in _____

Moses led the Israelites _to_ the Promised Land; Joshua led them _into_ the Promised Land. Both had God-given assignments that blossomed from their relationship and trust in God and their personal investment in each other.

Moses was the greatest man of God since Abraham. Just as Abraham taught an infant nation about faith, Moses taught an adolescent nation about law. One greater than any other would eventually come to teach not only Israel, but the world about a way stronger than law. The way of love and grace through giving His life as a final sacrifice so that all who believe in Him will be saved and ushered into the Eternal Promised Land. This "Joshua...Yeshua" is Jesus Christ.

154

At Billy Graham's funeral his daughter, Anne Graham Lotz, gave a beautiful memorial to her father that fits perfectly with this chapter of our study. The link is below and hopefully will remain viable for a long time. It is well worth its six minutes length to listen. (https://www.youtube.com/watch?v=d3p0KZN585M)

"So be strong and courageous! Do not be afraid and do not panic before them. For the Lord your God will personally go ahead of you. He will neither fail you nor abandon you." (Deuteronomy 31:6)

Just as God had gone before the Israelites in a cloud by day and pillar of fire by night, so Jesus promised the Holy Spirit would be in us and go before us, navigating our journey in this "foreign land" until we enter the Promised Land of Heaven forever, face to face with our precious Savior and Redeemer!

"Don't let your hearts be troubled. Trust in God, and trust also in me. There is more than enough room in my Father's home. If this were not so, would I have told you that I am going to prepare a place for you? When everything is ready, I will come and get you, so that you will always be with me where I am. And you know the way to where I am going."

Jesus told him, "I am the way, the truth, and the life. No one can come to the Father except through me.

"If you love me, obey my commandments. And I will ask the Father, and he will give you another Advocate, who will never leave you. He is the Holy Spirit, who leads into all truth. The world cannot receive him, because it isn't

looking for him and doesn't recognize him. But you know him, because he lives with you now and later will be in you. No, I will not abandon you as orphans—I will come to you.

"I am leaving you with a gift—peace of mind and heart. And the peace I give is a gift the world cannot give. So don't be troubled or afraid. Remember what I told you: I am going away, but I will come back to you again. If you really loved me, you would be happy that I am going to the Father, who is greater than I am." (John 14:1-4, 6, 15-18, 27-28)

"...and he has identified us as his own by placing the Holy Spirit in our hearts as the first installment that guarantees everything he has promised us." (2 Corinthians 1:22)

The Hope of the Resurrection. Getting from "here" to "there."

When we breathe our last breath in this body here on Earth, we will breathe our first breath in our new bodies in heaven. Death is part of life...and life is part of death. I can't help but think when we finally see the eternal home God has promised us, we will wonder why we resisted and held on so tightly to this world! The very word "death" can bring a chill of coldness, a sadness for those we leave behind. There is a finality in death...for this world. I get it. This world is what we see, feel, and experience. We try to relate our experience on earth with what heaven must be like, but it will pale in comparison to the realities of what it will be!

We must begin to look at death like we look at change. It's not what we are giving up but the beginning of new possibilities, hopes, promises fulfilled...life!

> *"I tell you the truth, those who listen to my message and believe in God who sent me have eternal life. They will never be condemned for their sins, but they have already passed from death into life. The Father has life in himself and he granted that same life-giving power to his Son...Indeed, the time is coming when all the dead in their graves will hear the voice of God's Son and they will rise again. Those who have done good will rise to experience eternal life, and those who have continued in evil will rise to experience judgment." (John 5:24,26-30)*

1Thessalonians 4:13-18

> *"And now, dear brothers and sisters, we want you to know what will happen to the believers who have died so you will not grieve like people who have no hope. For since we believe that Jesus died and was raised to life again, we also believe that when Jesus returns, God will bring back with him the believers who have died. We tell you this directly from the Lord: We who are still living when the Lord returns will not meet him ahead of those who have died. For the Lord himself will come down from heaven with a commanding shout, with the voice of the archangel, and with the trumpet call of God. First, the believers who have died will rise from their graves. Then, together with them, we who are still alive and remain on the earth will be caught up in the clouds to meet the Lord in the air. Then*

we will be with the Lord forever. So encourage each other with these words." (1 Thessalonians 4:13-18)

1 Corinthians 15

"But someone may ask, "How will the dead be raised? What kind of bodies will they have?" What a foolish question! When you put a seed into the ground, it doesn't grow into a plant unless it dies first. And what you put in the ground is not the plant that will grow, but only a bare seed of wheat or whatever you are planting. Then God gives it the new body he wants it to have. A different plant grows from each kind of seed.

It is the same way with the resurrection of the dead. Our earthly bodies are planted in the ground when we die, but they will be raised to live forever. Our bodies are buried in brokenness, but they will be raised in glory. They are buried in weakness, but they will be raised in strength. They are buried as natural human bodies, but they will be raised as spiritual bodies. For just as there are natural bodies, there are also spiritual bodies. The Scriptures tell us, "The first man, Adam, became a living person." But the last Adam—that is, Christ—is a life-giving Spirit. What comes first is the natural body, then the spiritual body comes later.

Just as we are now like the earthly man, we will someday be like the heavenly man. What I am saying, dear brothers and sisters, is that our physical bodies cannot inherit the Kingdom of God. These dying bodies cannot inherit what will last forever. But let me reveal to you a wonderful secret. We will not all die, but we will all be transformed! It will happen in a moment, in the blink of an eye, when the last trumpet is blown. For when the trumpet sounds, those who have died will be raised to live forever. And we who are living will also be transformed. For our dying bodies must be transformed into bodies that will never die; our mortal bodies must be transformed into immortal bodies. Then, when our dying bodies have been transformed into bodies that will never die, this Scripture will be fulfilled: "Death is swallowed up in victory. O death, where is your victory? O death, where is your sting? " For sin is the sting that results in death, and the law gives sin its power. But thank God! He gives us victory over sin and death through our Lord Jesus Christ. So, my dear brothers and sisters, be strong and immovable. Always work enthusiastically for the Lord, for you know that nothing you do for the Lord is ever useless." (1 Corinthians 15:35-38, 42-46, 49-58)

2 Corinthians 5

"For we know that when this earthly tent we live in is taken down (that is, when we die and leave this earthly body), we will have a house in heaven, an eternal body made for us by God himself and not by human hands. We grow weary in our present bodies, and we long to put on our heavenly bodies like new clothing. For we will put on heavenly bodies; we will not be spirits without bodies. While we live in these earthly bodies, we groan and sigh, but it's not that we want to die and get rid of these bodies that clothe us. Rather, we want to put on our new bodies so that these dying bodies will be swallowed up by life. God himself has prepared us for this, and as a guarantee

he has given us his Holy Spirit. So we are always confident, even though we know that as long as we live in these bodies we are not at home with the Lord. For we live by believing and not by seeing. Yes, we are fully confident, and we would rather be away from these earthly bodies, for then we will be at home with the Lord. So whether we are here in this body or away from this body, our goal is to please him. For we must all stand before Christ to be judged. We will each receive whatever we deserve for the good or evil we have done in this earthly body." (2 Corinthians 5:1-10)

Boundaries are not about exclusivity but reward, hope, life, freedom, and safety to anyone willing to sacrifice his own path for one that is better.

Do you know this Jesus as Savior and Lord?

God created a perfect man, Adam, and placed him in a perfect environment, the Garden of Eden. God initiated relationship with Adam, His creation. Adam, not God, broke that relationship when he chose sin over obedience. Ever since man has tried to work his way, counting his own goodness or morals as worthy to enter God's eternal home. Because of sin, perfection was destroyed.

Sin came with a price tag of death. God told Adam, "*You may freely eat of the fruit of every tree in the garden – except the tree of the knowledge of good and evil. If you eat its fruit, you are*

160

sure to die." (Genesis 2:16). Adam knew this warning before Eve was created. Sin entered the world through Adam's disobedience and Eve's deception.

Death entered the world through sin, and life would need to enter the world through death. But not just any death. This death would put an end to sin's domain (Romans 6:6-7) and replace a stony and stubborn heart with a clean, tender, and responsive heart (Ezekiel 36:26-27).

> *"...Yes, by God's Grace, Jesus tasted death for everyone. So now Jesus and the ones he makes holy have the same Father. That is why Jesus is not ashamed to call them his brothers and sisters.*
>
> *Because God's children are human beings—made of flesh and blood—the Son also became flesh and blood. For only as a human being could he die, and only by dying could he break the power of the devil, who had the power of death. Only in this way could he set free all who have lived their lives as slaves to the fear of dying.*
>
> *Therefore, it was necessary for him to be made in every respect like us, his brothers and sisters, so that he could be our merciful and faithful High Priest before God. Then he could offer a sacrifice that would take away the sins of the people."* (Hebrews 2:9,11, 14-15, 17)

God, not man, set the standard for restoring the relationship.

> *"For it is not possible for the blood of bulls and goats to take away sins. That is why, when Christ came into the*

world, he said to God, "You did not want animal sacrifices or sin offerings. But you have given me a body to offer. You were not pleased with burnt offerings or other offerings for sin.

For God's will was for us to be made holy by the sacrifice of the body of Jesus Christ, once for all time."

"For by that one offering he forever made perfect those who are being made holy.

And when sins have been forgiven, there is no need to offer any more sacrifices.

By his death, Jesus opened a new and life-giving way through the curtain into the Most Holy Place...let us go right into the presence of God with sincere hearts fully trusting him. For our guilty consciences have been sprinkled with Christ's blood to make us clean, and our bodies have been washed with pure water." (Hebrews 10:4-6, 10, 14, 18, 20, 22)

The restoration of mankind's relationship with God cost Jesus His life. Amazingly, God knew this relationship would be severed even before the beginning of time, before He created Adam!

"It was the precious blood of Christ, the sinless, spotless Lamb of God. God chose him as your ransom long before the world began..." (1 Peter 1:19-20)

This is why Jesus could claim, *"I am the way the truth and the life. No one can come to the Father except through me." (John 14:6)*

Our sin has been paid in full...once for all by Jesus Christ. He took the penalty of death upon Himself so we wouldn't have to. No can escape "physical death." We were never designed to live forever in these mortal bodies. The death Jesus paid for us is the second death, eternal death.

> *"And just as each person is destined to die once and after that comes judgment, so also Christ was offered once for all time as a sacrifice to take away the sins of many people. He will come again, not to deal with our sins, but to bring salvation to all who are eagerly waiting for him."* (Hebrews 9:27-28)

Someone had to pay for our sins (Romans 3:23-24; 6:23). When we breathe our last here on earth and open our eyes, standing before God, we will either stand before Him:

- "Sins paid in full"...our acceptance of Jesus Christ as the Son of God which gains us entry into God's eternal Kingdom, eternal home of Heaven.

OR

- Rejection of Jesus as the Son of God and His sacrifice which will then gain us entry into the kingdom of darkness, an eternity void of the presence and peace of God, an eternity of weeping and gnashing of teeth in hell.

Oh, I pray you choose wisely! Today is the day of salvation. No one is guaranteed a tomorrow. Our decision must be made while we are living today. Once we breathe our last breath on earth, time has run out, and our choice is made by default of death.

John 3:3,16-18, 36

"Jesus replied, 'I tell you the truth, unless you are born again, you cannot see the Kingdom of God'."

"For this is how God loved the world: He gave his one and only Son, so that everyone who believes in him will not perish but have eternal life. God sent his Son into the world not to judge the world, but to save the world through him. 'There is no judgment against anyone who believes in him. But anyone who does not believe in him has already been judged for not believing in God's one and only Son.

And anyone who believes in God's Son has eternal life. Anyone who doesn't obey the Son will never experience eternal life but remains under God's angry judgment'."

Romans 10:9

"If you confess with your mouth that Jesus is Lord and believe in your heart that God raised him from the dead, you will be saved. For it is by believing in your heart that you are made right with God, and it is by confessing with your mouth that you were saved."

Romans 5:1,6

"Therefore, since we have been made right in God's sight, by faith, we have peace with God because of what Jesus Christ our Lord has done for us. When we were utterly helpless, Christ came at just the right time and died for us sinners."

Acts 4:10, 12

"Let me clearly state to all of you and all the people of Israel that he was healed by the powerful name of Jesus Christ the Nazarene, the man you crucified but whom God

raised from the dead. There is salvation in no one else! God has given no other name under heaven by which we must be saved."

1 John 4:9-10, 5:1, 11-13

"God showed how much he loved us by sending his one and only Son into the world so that we might have eternal life through him. This is real love—not that we loved God, but that he loved us and sent his Son as a sacrifice to take away our sins."

"Everyone who believes that Jesus is the Christ has become a child of God...And everyone who loves the Father loves his children, too. And this is what God has testified: He has given us eternal life, and this life is in his Son. Whoever has the Son has life; whoever does not have God's Son does not have life. I have written this to you who believe in the name of the Son of God, so that you may know you have eternal life."

Have you accepted Jesus as the Son of God, the One who paid for your sins? If not, you can do so right now...right where you are. In fact, I'll pray with you:

Dear Jesus,

Thank you for coming into this world specifically to die for my sins and give me the amazing gift of eternal life. I accept what You did for me, and from this day forward I call you my Savior and Lord of my life. I surrender my heart and life to You. Teach me Your ways and Truths through Your Word.

In Jesus' Name I ask and accept...Amen

And so ends our journey…..or does it? I love Joshua 21:43-45 (bold type added):

> "So the Lord gave to Israel all the land he had sworn to their ancestors, and they took possession of it and settled there. And the Lord gave them rest on every side just as he had solemnly promised their ancestors. None of their enemies could stand against them, for the Lord helped them conquer all their enemies. **Not a single one of the good promises the Lord had given to the family of Israel was left unfulfilled; everything he had spoken came true.**"

OUR NEW HOME

"Then death and the grave were thrown into the lake of fire. This lake of fire is the second death. And anyone whose name was not found recorded in the Book of Life was thrown into the lake of fire." (Revelation 20:14-15)

"Then I saw a new heaven and a new earth, for the old heaven and the old earth had disappeared. And the sea was also gone. And I saw the holy city, the new Jerusalem, coming down from God out of heaven like a bride beautifully dressed for her husband. I heard a loud shout from the throne, saying, "Look, God's home is now among his people! He will live with them, and they will be his people. God himself will be with them. He will wipe every tear from their eyes, and there will be no more death or sorrow or crying or pain. All these things are gone forever.

"I saw no temple in the city, for the Lord God Almighty and the Lamb are its temple. And the city has no need of sun or moon, for *the glory of God illuminates the city, and the Lamb is its light."*

"The nations will walk in its light, and the kings of the world will enter the city in all their glory. Its gates will never be closed at the end of day because there is no night there."

"Nothing evil will be allowed to enter, nor anyone who practices shameful idolatry and dishonesty—but only those whose names are written in the Lamb's Book of Life."

(Revelation 21:1-4, 22-25, 27)

"No longer will there be a curse upon anything. For the throne of God and of the Lamb will be there, and his servants will worship him. And they will see his face, and his name will be written on their foreheads. And there will be no night there—no need for lamps or sun—for the Lord God will shine on them. And they will reign forever and ever. Then the angel said to me, 'Everything you have heard and seen is trustworthy and true. The Lord God, who inspires his prophets, has sent his angel to tell his servants what will happen soon. "Look, I am coming soon! Blessed are those who obey the words of prophecy written in this book. "

"Look, I am coming soon, bringing my reward with me to repay all people according to their deeds."

"Blessed are those who wash their robes. They will be permitted to enter through the gates of the city and eat the fruit from the tree of life."

"The Spirit and the bride say, 'Come.' Let anyone who hears this say, 'Come.' Let anyone who is thirsty come. Let anyone who desires drink freely from the water of life."

"He who is the faithful witness to all these things says, 'Yes, I am coming soon!' Amen! Come, Lord Jesus!" (Revelation 22:3-7, 12, 14, 17, 20)

Our great God,
this isn't just an amazing story of a
journey that started with the
life of one man, Abraham. But it is a
story of hope, faith, love, obedience, and
consequences that we can learn from
today in our life journey with You, oh
God, our faith journey with You.
And in all of our faults, our ups and
downs, our questioning where You are,
what You were doing in our lives,
direction in guidance where and what
we are to be doing and going, God You
are as faithful to us today as You were to
Abraham, Moses, Joshua, David, and all
the heroes of the faith.
We can trust that Your promises are true
to us today and that all of Your promises
to us will be fulfilled.
Amen

NOTES

Made in the USA
Middletown, DE
03 November 2020